WOMANISH
HOW SHE SURVIVED

Angelia Vernon Menchan

Honorable Menchan Media

2016©

#JUSTLOVE
#WOMANISH

I am a woman and was raised by women. My mom was a single woman of thirty when I was born and immediately I was thrust and immersed into the culture of women, my single mother, widowed grandmother, married godmother, two married aunts, one widowed aunt, one divorced aunt and another single aunt.

My grandmother bore ten children, six of whom were women, my mom two women children, two aunts one woman child and one man child, three aunts no children and my godmother one woman child.

In their presence I learned what it meant to be a woman in all its permeations. I have also spent most of my life in the presence of myriad women who shared through words or actions their lives with me, leaving me feel honored.

These stories aren't about us, me or my people and yet they are because as women we share so many similar experiences in such different ways.

1. *Her Unempowerment*

She was known as 'that woman'. Everyone who met her thought of her as beautiful, cutting edge stylish and raw. Those attributes were unheard of for a woman born in 1940, well stylish and beautiful were but raw not as much. They thought her raw because she drank hard and her conversation was peppered with expletives, in fact, one former friend described her as class with a filthy mouth and she embraced the image. She was also known for coming downtown in her day clothing and hours later showing up again dressed for the evening.

Men found Betta to be everything black men dreamed of at the time, she had light skin, was thin but shapely and could be sexy without trying. Many men vied for her attention throughout her late teens through her thirties but she ultimately became involved with a violent man, who thought he owned her. At age thirty-nine she was running for her life from one violent man, straight into the arms of another…

She was petrified. Roy told her he would kill her before he would let her go. She appealed to him, telling him he had a wife and kids to think about but he didn't seem to care. He was obsessed with her. When she met him she hadn't known he had a wife because he lived in the town over an hour away. He was well-dressed, mean looking and had pockets full of cash. He owned two huge trucks and was a savvy businessman, though not educated. By then she was in her late thirties and tired of simply being, that woman, she wanted to be taken care of. For the past eighteen years she worked in a clothing store as a saleswoman and made enough to house and feed herself but just that. Roy was in her mind the man of her dreams, and the sex blew her away. Sometimes he was gentle and other times less than gentle but she loved that. However, when she discovered he was married, she told him bye but he wouldn't allow her to leave, showing up at her store and home and forcing her to give into him. She grew to fear him and when she left town once without telling him, he choked her almost unconscious when she returned. From that point, things escalated and he became more obsessed and close to violent in his lovemaking. She had to get away.

One night they were at smoky nightclub and a big, dark man walked in and the crowds parted as if he were a god. Even Roy shrank a bit in his presence. Betta noticed how Roy deferred to him and felt a spark of something, something she couldn't identify. She didn't look at him long because Roy was always watching who she was watching. "Betta.." Roy barked and she stood, slowly making her way to him. The man watched her, his eyes taking her in but her eyes stayed focused on Roy. She was wearing a red dress Roy had purchased for her, with brown silk heels and her long, curly hair waved over her shoulder. Arriving at them, she made a point to stand close to Roy.

"John, this is Betta, Betta, this is John Jenkins, one of the first colored men to own several big rigs." Betta cringed inside at the word colored. It was 1978, and the word was Black.

"Betta is an unusual name." John said, his eyes piercing hers. She forced herself not to look directly into his eyes.

"It is actually Robetta but I was always called Betta. I think I was supposed to be Roberta but the spelling got messed up." John laughed and Roy dug his fingers into the flesh on her side. She knew that meant she was talking too much. Nodding, she made her way back to her table. She was aware she would pay later for whatever transgression Roy thought she was guilty of.

That night he had rough sex with her, so rough she cried out in pain. Rolling over after he was pleased, he looked up at the ceiling.

"You belong to me and I will kill you if you leave me." Sucking down sobs, she didn't say anything. Long after he was gone, she lay awake thinking she had sold her soul to the devil with no stairway to heaven.

~~YYYYY~~

Two days later, she was walking from the store to take a break and John blocked her, she stepped back as if afraid. He looked down at her, his eyes penetrating her. Lifting her chin with his fingers, he made her stare at him. His touch burned into her skin.

"You are too damn fine to be scared. Who hurt you?" She couldn't speak she was so filled with tears and fear. Taking her arm, he led her around the building and opened his truck for her. It was a huge truck but inside it was nice and roomy, and warm. It felt almost womblike to her. Climbing in on the passenger side, John turned to her, daring her not to look fully at him.

"Is Roy hurting you?" He asked. She nodded affirmatively. "I will take care of it. You will hear from me in a few days."

"I don't..."

"Shhh... trust me." He said, placing a kiss on his forehead.

She would always remember the desire that raced through her and that his lips were slightly chapped and his mustache thick. Getting out of the truck with his assistance, she looked up at him and he handed her a fifty-dollar bill. Puzzlement filled her eyes. She didn't want to be known as a woman who took money for mere kisses.

"Go get yourself some lunch and some eye drops, you are too pretty to have red eyes." She smiled slightly and made her way to the corner retail shop that also had a restaurant. They had cafeteria-style food. She suddenly felt hungry and hopeful. She ordered meatloaf and vegetables.

YYYYY

Three days later, she was going out with John. She was frightened but the day before he stopped by her store and assured her things were fine and he and Roy had come to an understanding. He also told her to wear red because that was her color and the color she was wearing when he met her. Again he gave her money, this time two hundred dollars.

That night when he arrived, he was in that huge truck and she was a bit taken aback but she didn't say anything. He was dressed in a dark brown suit with brown alligator shoes and a red shirt. He was also freshly shaven. He smelled like a barbershop, of bay rum and soap. He looked her over and winked at her.

Walking into the club the first person she saw was Roy and her heart raced. John placed his hand on the small of her back, as reassurance. She then noticed Roy's wife Ethel was with him. He never took Ethel out. Ethel was the same complexion as Betta but was shorter and heavier and walked with a limp as if one leg were shorter than the other. She was also dressed in red and her wavy hair was cut short. Her ears, wrists and fingers sparkled with diamonds. Betta knew who she was but wasn't sure if Ethel knew her. Taking her hand, John led her to Roy and Ethel. Betta felt as if she would faint, nausea filling her belly.

"Good evening Roy, it's good to see your beautiful wife tonight." Roy nodded but didn't look at Betta. Ethel smiled broadly.

"Every now and then he brings this old broad out. There was a time when I was with him all the time but lately not so much. I became a grandmother and that's my best job." Ethel said exuberantly as if she were genuinely thrilled to be there.

She was probably fifteen years older than Betta and maybe five years older than Roy. Rumor had it that her money from her parents when they died paid for Roy's trucks and she was the brains behind the operation because Roy wasn't an educated man. Roy still didn't say anything and John led Betta to a table. She sat and asked John what happened and a look of annoyance flit across his face.

"That's men's business. Just know you are safe now. As long as you are with me, you are safe." He said in a hard tone, filled with finality.

Betta didn't say anything. She knew she didn't want to be beholden to anyone but she was grateful for whatever John had done. She owed him. She just wasn't sure if she could afford to pay.

~~YYYYY~~

For more than six months, John took Betta around town as his woman. He didn't come to her house, they didn't have sex or become intimate, and he simply treated her like someone he was wooing. After a couple of months she relaxed into knowing she was safc from Roy and her feelings for John grew. He was a simple man who worked and loved to drink and eat good food on the weekends. He only drank on Fridays and Saturdays. On Sunday, though he didn't go to church, he rested.

Betta spent her time working and with her mother and two sisters; usually at one of their homes but no longer went out alone without John. Her sister Evalina, who was four years older than her was concerned about her growing relationship with John and mentioned it to her one night when they were all at Betta's having food and drinks. Her young sister, Birdie didn't say or do much other than work and take care of their mother.

"Betta, I hope you aren't jumping out the frying pan into the fire with this man."

"What does that mean?" Betta asked as she stood at the stove frying pork chops.

"Roy was a mean man, through and through. If he is scared of John, what must John be like? I heard he did time in Georgia for killing a man before he moved here. He only did about ten years and he has been out about twenty five but still…"

Betta hadn't heard anything. People didn't talk to her like that because other than people she was involved with or her sisters she was known to not mingle and would cuss those out who crossed her; especially those who tried getting in her business.

"I don't know if that's true or not but Evalina, he has been good to me. He hasn't made any sexual moves or anything. He takes me out for drinks and food and we have gone to the drive-in. If he did his time and has been free all those years, I'm not judging the man." Evalina sucked her teeth.

She liked men as much as her sister did but she chose better. The men she dated were almost passive because she was not dealing with cheats or abusive men. Her husband died in his fifties a few years ago making her a forty-year-old widow. She

15

didn't have children, and neither did her sisters and neither Betta nor Birdie had ever married. In fact, Birdie who was a nurse still lived with their mother.

"I don't expect you to listen to me and I know you like 'em big, black and hard and he is sure enough that but he is just slicker with his mean shit but go on. I just don't know why you got rid of one and fell into another and you might want to ask why he isn't dicking you down. There has to be a reason. Either his thing doesn't work, he is giving it to someone else or he is setting you up. You are half in love with him already and if he is good at dicking you gon' fall right into his damn trap and when it happens remember I told you so."

Betta placed the pork chops on a paper towel to drain before taking them to the table. She had placed sliced tomatoes, sweet onions, pickles, and homemade bread out and they were drinking Seagram's Seven and Seven up.

Halfway through the meal, they heard a knock on the door and Betta went to answer. It was John and he was dressed in his work clothing. A smile lit her face up at the sight of him. He had been on the road for two days.

"Hey…"

"Hey baby, I was passing by and decided to stop." Evalina snorted. She figured his ass was spying when he saw a car parked outside other than Betta's.

"Come on in, Evalina and Birdie are here."

"Nah, I need to shower and sleep. I will stop by tomorrow."

"Wait, let me get you a plate." She rushed to the kitchen, filled a plate with food, and handed it to him.

Smiling, he looked down at her taking the plate. When she returned to the kitchen she told Evalina not to say a damn word and she didn't. She had said what she came to say.

¥¥¥¥¥

The next evening John showed up at Betta's dressed in starched jeans and a white shirt. That was another look she never saw. She was wearing a red summer dress with white flowers and flat white sandals. She had gotten dressed, not knowing when he would arrive. She prepared a meal. She invited him in and he followed her to the kitchen. Her house was small and the rooms ran right into the other. The kitchen and dining room were separated from the living room by a bookshelf filled with books. There were also two bedrooms, a bathroom, and a closed in back porch that served as a laundry and storage area.

"It smells good in here." He said, taking at seat at the small table where the sisters sat the night before. He looked huge sitting there. She quickly washed her hands and filled his plate with roasted chicken, green beans and yams, food she knew most men liked. She filled hers and sat down across from him. He blessed the food and they started eating. He cleared half his plate before looking up at her.

"You can really cook Betta, no wonder men are going mad over you."

"It isn't the cooking, you are the only man I ever cooked for."

"What is it Betta?" He asked. There was something to his tone that made her censor what she would naturally say. She instinctively knew John wouldn't appreciate her mentioning her sexual appetite with other men to him.

"I hope it's me. What else could it be?" She said and he grinned at her.

"Right you are." He said. "I have taken my time with you. I know you were in a situation with Roy and I had a couple of situations myself. I tied up my loose ends and I feel you have also. I have two sons. One is in prison and the other one is a sissy."

"A sissy?" She was appalled John would call his own flesh a sissy but she wasn't sure why she felt that way, refined was not who John was.
"Yes, my ex married a man they say messed with him and now he is a sissy. He is walking around in dresses and shit but he's my son. He don't bother

me much but sometimes he comes by and asks me for money and I give it to him. The other one is going to be locked up forever. He killed a cop."

Her blood ran cold at the information and the nonchalant way he said it. He stood and took her hand, leading her to her bedroom. Her heart thumped in her chest. John pulled the hairpins from her hair and watched her curls unravel around her shoulders. He then slowly undressed her until she stood before him naked. She had never been more self-conscious in her life. She knew she was in great shape but she was a hairy woman and her mons, thighs and stomach was covered with soft fine hair. His eyes darkened at the sight of her and he sat on the bed and started licking her stomach. Heat flew threw her like scalding hot water. No man had ever placed his mouth on her body except her lips, neck and nipples. Pulling her down on the bed, he opened her legs and stood over her admiring the view.

"You look like a real black woman. Your body is like god made it and you aren't shaving and trying to take on the ways of the white woman." She was so glad in that moment she had not shaved.

Getting on his knees, he started kissing her all over her lower body and when he started to perform oral love on her, she literally screeched. Glancing up at her, he continued his journey of her body and she knew she was lost to him forever. By the time he undressed and entered her, she was ready for all he had and he was abundant. He was as talented with making love as with his tongue and he made love to her several times that night. Sometimes he was gentle, other times he was rough, almost brutal but she loved every minute of it.

The next morning he told her to get up and get dressed, because they were getting married.

Three hours later, they were done at the Justice of the Peace and back home, to his house, a big rambling house he was fixing up.

YYYYY

The first time he hit her they were married almost two years. After getting married she settled into being John's wife. He made her quit work and he saw she had everything she needed and wanted. Many women, including her sisters envied how much John provided for her. He quickly built her a big stone home in the country and she could shop and get her hair done as often as she liked. Her hair is what made him hit her.

"I want my haircut in a bob." Betta told the hairstylist. It was summer and she was now forty and her thick heavy hair weighed her down. With reluctance the stylist cut inches of her hair, leaving the back short but the front and sides swinging against her jawline.

John stopped when he walked in the door and saw her hair. He walked up to her and lifted her hair and just as quickly backhanded her across the face, sending her sprawling to the floor. In shock she lay sprawled on the floor staring up at him. Blood oozed from the side of her nose. Offering his hand, he reached down, pulling her up. Once on her feet, she snatched away from him and backed into the kitchen. He looked at her before apologizing.

"I'm sorry baby but you cut off your crown and glory. You can't change yourself and expect it to be okay." He said.

"Are you kidding? This is my hair and it's 1980."

"I don't want to hear any of that white woman shit in my house either. What year it is has nothing to do with nothing. I don't want you cutting your hair and that's that. I'm going to take a shower."

He stepped out of the room and she dropped down in a chair. All of the changes that had occurred filled her mind, she no longer had girl's nights with her sisters and he was always with her when she visited her mom. Her dresses were still red but he had once commented on how tight they were and she started purchasing them looser. He had completely taken over her life. He gave her everything but was it enough for what he asked in return?

"Betta…" hearing his voice made her jump up and race to the bedroom. He was sitting on the side of the bed, naked.

Though in his fifties, John's body was hard and muscular and she could see his desire. She hadn't even washed the blood off her face. He pulled her down on the bed and gently cleaned her face with his damp towel. He then undressed her and slowly started seducing her. She willed her body not to respond but it betrayed her and she gave into his skilled lovemaking.

<del>YYYYY</del>

For ten years Betta was a battered and emotionally beaten woman. He didn't hit her often but when he did it became progressively worse. She suffered a broken wrist once for waving at a man, another time he stepped on her foot, crushing the bones because she danced too 'nasty' at a family party. There were also blackened eyes and busted lips for random and imagined doings. John had done just what her sister warned years ago, he had bought and paid for her and damaged her with beatings and sex to keep her his slave.

Neither her mother nor her sisters were ever able to reach her. They also felt they didn't know her. She had changed from a vibrant, beautiful woman who spoke her mind to one who was brittle and afraid who looked as if life had been sucked from her. She was also bloated from the alcohol they consumed together regularly. Their intimacy was sex and liquor. She was still his obsession but he had become her jailer who battered her body before soothing it with sex.

YYYYY

Evalina insisted on Betta having a fiftieth birthday party. She and their mom convinced John to allow it. Fiftieth birthdays were a big deal in their family and everyone on the block was invited. The birthday girl only had to dress and show up.

That morning Betta woke up and sat at her dresser assessing herself. She was still a good-looking woman but she looked tired and old and her long curly hair was streaked with grey. Something inside her unraveled and she made a decision she was going to get a haircut, get her eyebrows arched and her nails painted. She was also going to wear a black dress. That was something she hadn't done in years. She didn't allow herself to think of what John would say. That suddenly didn't matter either. She told him she would meet him at her sisters for the party and went to take care of herself.

When Betta arrived at Evalina's, Evalina and Birdie stopped speaking and their mouths opened in shock. Betta's hair was dark brown, short and curly and her brows were done and she was dressed in a black dress that was snug but stopped halfway her calves. In two-inch heels, she looked amazing. Tears flew from Evalina's eyes and she wasn't one who cried.

"Lord Betta, you look like your old self. Hello fifty." Betta smiled and took a seat at the table with her sisters. They were also dressed and ready and food covered every surface in the kitchen. Someone had set up the music outside and there were tents and chairs.

"Thank you, I woke up this morning and decided it was time. Where is mama?"

"She is inside."

When John arrived, the party was in full throttle. The music played and people were laughing, talking and drinking. The sisters' mom was inside resting but had joined in on the birthday singing. He looked around for Betta and did a double take when he saw her. Swiftly making his way to her, he grabbed her arm, literally dragging her inside.

Once they were inside the hallway, he grabbed her by her hair, yanking it hard.

"What the hell is this, Betta? I don't know who talked you into it." She snatched away and backed up to a wooden desk.

"It is my fucking hair and I wanted to cut it and I did." Storming over to her, he slapped her across her face and she quickly pulled open the third drawer on the desk, pulled out the gun she knew was there and shot him at point blank range in the chest. A look of pure astonishment covered his face before he collapsed on the floor. Hearing the gunshot, Evalina and several others rushed in the house and found Betta standing over John with the gun in her hand and blood dripping from her lip. John lay in a puddle of blood, his eyes open and a stunned look still on his face.

"Oh my God Betta." Birdie screamed before fainting and Evalina went into action, calling the police and ambulance while taking the gun and helping Betta sit down. Betta looked as if she were in a trance.

The police arrived with the ambulance and John was announced dead. Betta hadn't uttered a word but her arms were wrapped around her body. The officer knew the family and took a statement from Evalina and several others who saw John snatch her inside. Her busted and bleeding lip was all the evidence needed to prove it was self-defense. They turned her over to Evalina.

After the police and ambulance was gone, Evalina filled a tub with water and helped her sister inside. Birdie had taken their mom home with her. Birdie didn't deal well with much and this was too much for her. Their mom who was in her eighties just wanted to make sure Betta was okay and not going to prison and becoming a bull-dagger. Evalina had wanted to shout with laughter when her mom said that but it wasn't the time for laughter. Several of the men had rolled up the rug John bled on and mopped the floor beneath it. It was as if it never were.

Evalina filled a glass with scotch for her sister and another for herself before sitting on the covered toilet. Betta took a huge sip, a lone tear trailing down her face as she sat in the hot water laced with lavender oils and Epsom salts.

"I killed him Evalina."

"I know baby. He had it coming."

"This morning when I got up I felt different. I looked in the mirror at myself and didn't like what I had become. He beat me and sexed me for ten years. That was my life and I didn't know what else I would have or do. I loved him Evalina like a sickness and because he was mostly so good to me, I allowed it. I feel like I got dressed to kill him and on my birthday."

The sisters sipped silently and when Betta drained her glass she handed it to Evalina to refill. She got out the tub, dried and moisturized before pulling on her sister's chenille bathrobe and joining her in the kitchen.

"Evalina what do you think is going to happen?" Betta asked. She sounded exhausted and frightened.

"Not much. Officer Jones said you will likely have to make an appearance but since we saw him drag you in here and since your mouth was busted it's clearly self-defense." Betta looked over at her sister and dread filled Evalina's belly. There was something in Betta's expression.

"It was self-defense but when he was dragging me into this room, I remembered this is where you kept that thirty-eight and said to myself if he hit me I was going to shoot his ass. He did and I did."

"Evalina let that be the last time you say that. Do you hear me?" Betta blinked back tears and drained her glass just as she had before. She had a third glass of scotch before crawling in bed with her sister and passing out. John's eyes were in her dreams.

YYYYY

Just as Evalina predicted there was an inquest a few days later and the shooting was ruled as self-defense. It was also revealed John had done time for killing a woman in Georgia and time for having beaten his son's mother unconscious.

Betta allowed Evalina to take care of everything, even getting John cremated. She certainly wasn't planning or going to the funeral of the man she killed.

A week later Betta discovered John left her an abundant amount of insurance money, property and a trucking business. She knew she would sell the trucking business and the property and would also give money to John's son who was not in prison. It was the right thing to do. What she needed to do more than anything was leave town, get away from everything she knew and grieve for John and for herself and what she had done and had to overcome.

YYYYY

Six weeks after shooting the man she loved who had beaten her, Betta, filled with sadness, fled town. She sold the business to Roy of all people and much of the property to others. She kept her home and the ten acres surrounding it. She needed to get away. She felt as if she would die if she stayed any longer. She ended up on a small island off the coast of Beaufort, South Carolina.

An island filled with black people who maintained much of the African culture. For several months she immersed herself fully in their culture, their medicines and religions until she felt whole, new and forgiven. Much of that time was spent in the company of women. Women who nurtured her, prayed for her, listened to her story in bits and pieces as she shared it. They also shared their food, recipes and taught her to make soap, how to preserve foods, how to quilt and how to live free from guilt. It was the best year of her life. When her sister called to say her mother was dying, she knew it was home going time.

¥¥¥¥¥

I met Betta a few years after she returned home. When she returned there were whispers and stares but her year of peace prepared her for that and she rarely noticed. She had come home to serve other women and that's what she did. She volunteered two days a week at Becoming Whole, a shelter for abused women and one day at the prison education center. The other days she filled with growing vegetables she gave away, reading and spending many evenings with her sister, Birdie who remained single. Evalina married an old beau who was widowed and moved to Augusta, Georgia but they spoke daily by phone.

There were men who approached her, even knowing her history but she had not become interested in that part of her life again. She was a stunning woman who was clear skinned, clear eyed and very fit from her gardening and daily walks.

She had also not consumed any alcohol since the night she shot John.

I heard her speaking at Becoming Whole and was mesmerized by the way she stood with authority, the way she looked with her short silver hair cut down to the wave and the billowing yellow cotton dress she wore. Her words were ingrained on my consciousness.

"I killed my husband and I don't recommend that to anyone. My answer is to always find a way to leave. You that are here are ahead of the curve by coming to this great resource. I never did that. I loved him, I felt indebted to him and he made love to me like he created my body. I was lovesick in its purest definition. I didn't have any children and it was just me and I could have gotten on any train or bus and left but I stayed."

She paused to allow her words to sink in and resonate.

"The morning of the night I shot him, I woke up feeling different. I looked at myself and did not like what I saw. It was also my fiftieth birthday, four years ago. I went and cut my hair knowing he didn't like my hair short. When he saw me, he grabbed me in front of people attending my birthday party. When he hit me I pulled a gun from the drawer and shot him. I will never ever forget the stunned look on his face before he dropped."

The room was eerily silent. I raised my hand and she acknowledged me.

"Do you think he loved you although he hit you?"
Her eyes held mine and she spoke without hesitation.

"He loved me in the way he knew love to be. He married me, he didn't have other women, he provided for me above and beyond which means in his warped mind that gave him the authority to hit me when I got out of line. He felt love was ownership. I discovered after shooting him he killed one woman and almost killed another."

"Why did you feel indebted?" I asked. A smile played around her mouth.

"He saved me from another violent man I was seeing, as my grandmother used to say, I swapped the witch for the devil."

After she was done speaking she walked to me and asked if I had any other questions. I literally wanted to race with excitement but instead I coolly thanked her and we sat down with tea.

"What do you do?" She asked. I told her I was employed, but I described myself as a self-employed social scientist, the term made her laugh.

"What did you do after shooting him?" I asked.

"I don't really remember the first couple of hours. My sisters got rid of the guests and took my mom away after it happened. I do recall my oldest sister taking care of me and everything else for John's services. It didn't really hit me that I killed him until I stood before the judge. After a couple of weeks, I fled. Of course people were whispering, some I'm sure thought I killed him for the land, insurance money and house. I knew John owned the trucks but I didn't have a clue about the property other than our home and I certainly never thought hc had a huge insurance policy. He was so archaic about women."

"Perhaps, that's why he had it. He wanted to control and take care of you after death." I offered. Full-throated laughter burst forth from her.

"You are a smart one. How old are you?"

"I'm thirty one."

"Oh to be thirty one and so smart. Are you married?"

"Yes, with two children." Something changed in her face at the word children. I chose not to venture there.

"John had two sons. One is in prison for life and the other died last year from AIDS. I didn't know either one. The one who died visited a few times when we were married and after John died, I gave him money."

"What would you do differently?" I asked. She closed her eyes, as if she could only gather her thoughts that way.

"Oh, so many things! I would respect myself more as a younger woman. I would not give away so much of me to men who only wanted me because I was very sexual and provocative. I would never, ever have gotten involved with a married man whom I had to be protected from by another man. I would never allow a man to fight my battles because often what I owe is so much more than what I gained."

Her eyes flew open and they were glassy and vulnerable. I felt her pain and her growth and I was so glad she spoke with me. I also knew she had nothing else to say and I had nothing else to ask. I also knew for sure, she was a blessing to those she was now serving.

2. *I Had His Children... He Didn't Put A Ring On It*

"I'm pregnant." She told him, sitting in his car far away from the city. He was thirty to her twenty-two and he was the only man she ever had sex with. He was so handsome and used to call her his pretty wallflower. She was the only girl of seven children and the youngest. Her brothers protected her virtue. Her mom worked hard as a housekeeper and her dad died when she was twelve leaving her brothers filling his shoes. One of them took her to school until she graduated at seventeen and collectively they paid for her to attend college at Florida Memorial.

A year ago when she graduated, they were all there in attendance, the older four with their wives and children and the younger two, both military men, were there on leave. Their mom passed away suddenly two years earlier at sixty and her

44

graduation was a cause for celebration. To them she was Sissy and they were proud of her. She was starting a nursing internship the following week.

The first time she saw Carlos Henry was that night at a party for the graduates and he looked like his name. His complexion was almost golden and he had a thin mustache with nice lips and dreamy eyes. He was beautiful. Especially to a woman who didn't see her own beauty. Sissy was lovely with flawless dark skin, soulful, almost black eyes and a small mole above her lip that added to her allure, but she saw it as ugly and thought her lips and eyes too large for her face. She also had an abundance of hair she tamed with a straightening comb. Standing against the wall she couldn't stop staring at him. Feeling her eyes he turned to stare at her and was taken with her innocent beauty. She was wearing a white dress that enhanced more than hid her very shapely body. Her breasts and hips were abundant her waist small. He wanted to *wrap his hands around her waist and pull her close to him. He knew her brothers and knew to proceed with caution. Looking around he saw the two who were sailors dancing and assumed the others were gone. He made his way to her.*

"Would you like to dance ma'am?" He asked.

Sissy looked around as if to see who he was talking to. Grinning at her in that lopsided way she would come to love, he took her hand, pulling her onto the floor and was stunned at how well she danced. She danced naturally and beautifully as if she were a different person. They ended up dancing several times before her brother Nathan, the closest to her in age at twenty-four, appeared at her side.

"Sissy, Bernard told me to take you home when I got ready to leave." He ignored Carlos. Smiling shyly, she nodded at Carlos and followed her

brother. Once they were in the car, Bernard started.

"That dude is a player and he's too old for you. Stay away from him Sissy. I'm warning you. They also say he has some kind of strange relationship with his mama. You know that old lady with yards of hair who lives in that big old haunted looking house."

Sissy didn't respond. She stared out the window thinking of how Carlos felt next to her, his hard erection on her thigh and the scent of tobacco on his jacket. She was a virgin with an active sexual fantasy life. She knew that tomorrow she was picking up her new car and would start her new job as a nurse for Dr. Lance, a Negro gynecologist. The small house she grew up in was now hers and she was a grown woman. She didn't need her brothers' protection or money any longer.

47

~~YYYYY~~

After a month of working, Sissy allowed Geneva, another practical nurse to convince her to go to the Club Diana on Friday night. Sissy had never been to a club and was scared but thrilled. She loved dancing and was a great dancer though most of her dancing was done in dance class and in the privacy of her own bedroom. She planned to have fun that night. Her youngest brothers were back at their duty stations and the older four were busy with work and family. No one really had the time to see what Sissy was doing and for that she was very grateful.

Walking in, she felt glamorous in her black satin dress that hugged her body and her red and black pumps. Carlos spotted her the minute she walked in and could sense her discomfort. She was with a woman he saw often in bars and clubs and was surprised Sissy was with her. He watched her follow Geneva to a table and the waiter arrived to take their orders. Carlos smiled when he saw the waiter return with two glasses filled with ice, a ginger ale, and two small bottles of gin. He knew the soft drink was for Sissy. He watched her for over an hour and not once did she get asked to dance. Pushing up off the counter he made his way to her.

"Hello Wallflower." Her face warmed at his words.

"My name is Sistora Woodbine but my friends call me Sissy." She whispered.
"I'm going to call you Wallflower, my pretty wallflower."
Pulling out a chair, he turned it around sitting with his legs open, draped around the chair, staring at her. "You're always by the wall and you're as

pretty as a flower." Nervously, Sissy picked up her glass, gulping down her beverage.

"I want to know you Sissy. What do you do?"

"I'm a nurse for Dr. Lance. I got my first pay today." She blurted. He grinned at her.

"That's a good job. I'm a foreman at Dickeys; the first Negro foreman. I have a diploma."

It was 1958 and Sissy was impressed. Her older brothers had all dropped out of school to work and her younger ones joined the military without diplomas though Bernard had gotten one later. She was the first in her family with a diploma and degree. "I have a son. He lives with his mama in Orlando. I live with my mom. She's seventy two."

"My parents are deceased. I have six brothers."

"I know the Woodbine brothers. They are known for being family oriented, hardworking men's men. Good guys. Can I take you for a drive?" He asked and fear and desire curled in her belly.

"I have my car."

*"I'll bring you back or I'll follow you home and
then we'll drive." She agreed and hurriedly told
Geneva who waved her on.*

*They ended up miles from town where he had a
cabin owned by his father. It was sparsely
furnished and clean but there was no electricity.
He quickly lit oil lamps and told her to have a seat.
The only seat was a bed and she quickly sat primly
on the edge of it. He stood in front of her and her
mouth went dry at his prominent erection.*

*Taking her hand, he pulled her up and covered her
mouth with his, licking her lips and slowly kissing
her. She felt electrocuted. She followed his
instruction, kissing him back. Pulling back, he
looked down at her.*

"You're a natural."

He lifted her dress and slowly and expertly unhooked her stockings, pulling them off with her shoes. She knew she should stop him but couldn't. He relieved her of her garter and panties before taking off her dress. She stood before him in her bra and half-slip. Pushing her on the bed, he lifted her slip and did something she had only imagined. He placed his mouth on her and started licking and slurping between her legs. She wanted to scream or die because it felt so good. Holding her tight he increased the tempo until she felt a tidal wave of feelings and exploded on his tongue, her body jerking in amazement, rendering her dazzled. He wouldn't stop his feast. She literally thought she would die of pleasure. When he finally stopped she lay on the bed, her legs open and arms akimbo. Standing, he sat beside her and lit a cigarette. Feeling exposed, she sat up and tried to cover herself.

"Don't hide. You're a woman. Be proud of that. I'm going to take my time with you Wallflower."

For the next seven months they spent every Friday and Saturday night in that cabin. All she did was work and wait for the weekends so he could feast on her and fill her with his thickness. She grew to crave the sex. Everything was perfect until she missed two periods.

He stared at her several minutes letting her words sink in.

"Pregnant? I thought your doctor gave you some sponge or something?"

"I guess it didn't work." She said, watching him and his demeanor change.

He stood pacing around before he turned to her.

"You can't have it. I told my mama I wouldn't have any more babies." She stared at him in shock. He was weeks away from his thirty-first birthday.

"Your mama?" A curl of derision filled her tone.

"Yea. I live with her. I'm all she's got and she's sickly. This might kill her." Sissy stood, brushing off her skirt.

"I'm having this baby. If your last child didn't kill her, neither will this one. Deal with your mama and I'll deal with my brothers."

Something hard solidified inside her. Her heart felt shredded like the lettuce in a taco but she would have her baby.

Sissy's brothers were infuriated and threatened to
kill Carlos but she told them if they said a word
she would leave and never return. They saw
something in her they never saw before. Sissy was
a grown woman who no longer needed anyone's
protection.

"I made a decision to be with him. He didn't rape
me or make me, I chose and I'm choosing to have
this baby. I have a job and a home and I will do
what I need to do." She told them and their wives
agreed with her, telling them to mind their own
business. A couple of them had been pregnant
when they married.

Carmelita Henry, Carlos' mother actually showed
up at Sissy's job calling her whore and slut and
several other names. Carmelita was a tall florid
woman dressed in widow's weeds as they were

called, which meant everything she wore was black and long. The contrast to her yards of silver hair and pale skin was startling. She also looked completely healthy.

"You are not good enough for Carlos. You are like the rest of these black sluts, always trying to trap a good man with your asses."

"Your son chased my ass and still is. Look around, you are in my place of employment which means I have a job and I also have a bought and paid for house which is more than I can say for your son. Leave or I will call the police." Sissy said quietly with authority. Carmelita stormed out her harsh words filling the air.

~~YYYYY~~

For the next seven months Sissy held her head high and worked until she went into labor. Carlos stopped by weekly with money, food and for sex until she was no longer able. He never spent a night and always went home to his mother. That became their life; Carlos visiting and returning home to Carmelita. He gave their daughter his name and three years later their son but he never married her. He was married to his mother. Sissy didn't feel taken advantage of because once she was over the pain of his initial rejection she saw it for what it was and he took care of what she had to.

YYYYY

Carmelita died at age ninety when Carlos was in his early fifties and Sissy in her mid-forties, their daughter was almost twenty-three and married and their son twenty in college. The night after the funeral Carlos asked Sissy to marry him and she laughed until tears poured. He never forgot her words until the day he died.

"Marry you? Why would I marry you now? My house is paid for, I'm making great money, my kids are grown and my bank account is flush. It's too late for marriage. I love my life just as it is." She reached over and took his ring, however, placing it on her right hand.

Not much changed in their lives for the next twenty-five years until Carlos died.

A week after the funeral Sissy and I spoke and of course I asked if she regretted never marrying anyone by waiting for Carlos.

"Damn right. For ten years I waited for marriage. I convinced myself he would man up and ask me but he never did. It took twenty-three years and the death of his mom. I had grown used to it all."

"Did you ever have sex with another man?"

"I sure did. More than one but not a damned one could make me feel like Carlos did. He savored me. He never slacked on how he savored me and I loved him. So I had his children and allowed him to be married to his mama. By the time he asked I no longer cared about marriage. What was the point?"

I had no idea. None at all.

3. *When I Married Him, I Didn't Love Him...*

She sat next to me in a women's faith class. She was a small woman of eighty who always wore a hat and some type of sweater. She also didn't look around and had a stern face but there was always a smile playing around her lips as if she knew secrets. For many months, I often hugged her but until she was in the class with me we never exchanged any words. Frankly, she reminded me of those church women who were judgmental and didn't like anyone much. However, I came to learn that I was the one doing the judging...

On the second day of the class we started talking about marriage and there were women from twenty-four to eighty at the table. We all gave input on our marriages and I was the one with the longest standing marriage, one woman in her fifties had been married almost twenty years, the mid-thirties woman was married five years and the youngest was divorced. The eldest one, Mary, was widowed.

After listening to all of us Mary said, quietly, "I didn't love my husband when I married him that came much later."

Being the social scientist I considered myself to be, I looked around at the faces of the other woman and there were varying degrees of surprise, in fact the young divorcee looked downright befuddled. My eyes found Mary and that smile had increased.

"There are more reasons to marry than for love and they are more lasting." She said. She did not get to elaborate with the class because the facilitator reengaged the class but afterwards I walked out with her and asked if she wanted coffee.

"No thanks but I will take some tea." She followed me downtown for coffee and tea and I asked her what she meant by her comment. Her eyes pierced mine and she stunned me with her question.

"You married for love, didn't you?"

"Yes ma'am."

"But I bet that wasn't your only consideration, was it?"

"No ma'am. He had to love me also, he had to be a good man who worked and placed his family first, and he had to be someone who valued me as more than his wife."

"I can see that on you. Here was my thing. I'm eighty years old and I dropped out of school and started working at the coffee factory. At that time I was sixteen and that was a mighty good job. I was raised by my grandmother, and when we turned sixteen we had to quit school and work. Mind you, this was 1950 and that's how it was. I was a good student but I understood how it worked. I started in the factory packing coffee in cans for nine years but in late 1959 they opened a couple of jobs for Negro women in the typing pool and I applied and got one of those jobs. I was a good typist. Mostly, those women made less but they didn't change my pay because I had been a good worker for years and saved up my money. I had me a nice little house and I was good. I also had me a man friend who came by a couple nights a week and they always had to leave money on the table. I wasn't selling love but it wasn't free either."

I was frothing inside with excitement. I loved stories from older women because they were never quite what we thought. There was always so much more banked inside them than what showed.

63

"I lived like that until I was about thirty seven, working and paying my own way. In 1971 they hired the first black manager. He was in his mid-forties and handsome if you liked a tall, quiet type man. I didn't pay him any attention either way. I figured I would be single all my life and having babies was off the table as far as I was concerned. One day I was walking to my car and it started raining and he hurried over with an umbrella and walked me to my car.

"Thank you." I said, once I was inside. He stood outside my car looking down at me from under the huge umbrella.

"You can thank me by letting me buy you supper." He said in a deep, well- modulated voice. I always had a weakness for deep voices that resonated.

"Okay." He told me to follow him to a small restaurant on Main Street and I did. We had dinner and he told me he was a widower with two sons, one twelve and the other fifteen. His wife had been dead for four years from cancer. To me he was just a nice man.

However, he asked me out several more times and we became friends, talking about work, his kids, goings on in the city and such. I invited him to church. After church I invited him home for dinner and as they say one thing led to the other. He was a quiet and serious man who was not quiet and serious in bed. He had not been with a woman in a couple of years and I was tired of the in and out of my relationships.

When he asked me to marry him five months later, I didn't fancy myself in love but I said yes because I looked at the big picture. He was a good man, he was great in bed, he had a good job and a nice big house and his sons liked me once they met me. Why not marry him? I read the bible and in the bible it tells a man to love his wife as Christ loves the church but not in one scripture does it require a woman to love her husband." My brow went up and she laughed. "Read it for yourself. It says submit and some other things but not one scripture says that. I was at a point in my life where I could submit. I had worked twenty years and saved my money, I had a house I could sell and have more money and he wanted me at home taking care of him and the boys. I was agreeable to all of that. We were married more than thirty five years before he died when he was eighty and I was seventy three."

"Did you love him by then?"

"I did. There was no big fall or swooning, or anything like that. I wasn't that kind of woman but one day he was working in the yard and fell from a ladder and I felt as if I couldn't breathe. I rushed to him and a neighbor called an ambulance. He had crushed the side of his head and lay in a coma for several days. I prayed like I never prayed in my life and I also knew in those days how much I loved him and how full my life was with him in it. When he recovered, I told him I loved him and we realized it was our twenty-second anniversary. He smiled telling me he had always loved me from the day he walked me to my car. We had thirteen more great years. He was retired, the boys were married and lived away and we traveled and lived our good life. I saw many of those hot in love relationships come and go. Many marriages got burned up by them."

I listened raptly and understood what she said, even if I didn't agree. I felt every woman; every person should get consumed by being in love and having someone in love with them at least once, maybe twice. But I also understood it took more than in love to sustain a marriage and hers had all that it took.

4. *He Was Mine First: A Story of Justification*

Her feet were on the coffee table, a can of beer beside her feet. Marcel curls covered her small head and she was clearly feeling no pain. There had been the consumption of several twelve-ounce cans of beer. The room smelled of women, black women: that scent of perfume, mixed with the sweetness of hair grease and a curl of smoke from a cigarette.

"I didn't want to marry him, so he married her. I got married and moved away but when I returned free, he became mine again." A couple of the women nodded but one woman asked 'the' question.

"What about his wife. He's been married to that woman for years. Doesn't she matter?"

Picking up her beer can, she took a sip, squinting at the audacity of the younger woman to question her. Placing the can on the table, she sat up, removing her feet from the table, squaring her shoulders. The younger woman flinched internally but didn't look away. She really wanted to know how the other woman felt.

"He was my man first..." She said emphatically as if that was the only answer necessary. Yet for the next answer she told her story, their story.

He walked in the bar and I noticed him immediately. He was tall and handsome and very well dressed with dark skin. All the things I like in a man. I knew who he was. He was arrogant and brash and though it was 1947, he had money. I never thought he would approach me, I was dark skinned, short with no curves to speak of but I had nice big breasts and my legs weren't bad. I also wore thick glasses but they were stylish. I was dressed though, always dressed. That night I was wearing a gold straight dress with satin heels and my lips were red. When I saw him stroll towards me, I turned away and picked up my glass filled with beer.

"You saw me..." He said and I felt his breath on my neck. He smelled like a man of spicy cologne and lifebuoy soap. I didn't turn to him but continued sipping my beer.

Walking around me, he took my glass from my hand and sat it on the counter before lifting my chin with three fingers.

"You saw me and you know I saw you. Come on let me take you for a ride." He said.

I didn't say anything but I picked up my beer and my purse and followed him. He drove to the Pimbleton Hotel, a nice hotel for Negroes. I looked

at him and he assured me I didn't have to do
anything I didn't want to. After several hours in his
presence I did everything I wanted to and he
wanted me to. I was twenty-six and enjoyed men
but no man ever touched me like that. He told me
that night he was my man and I was his woman.
He was widowed. His young wife died in
childbirth. He also told me he had other women.
He said it like it was normal and it was. I had
never known a faithful man, not even my father.

For six years we did what we did how we did and
he asked me to marry him. I asked if he would still
be him. He said he was offering me the house, the
car and him but also what we already had. The
women wouldn't stop and I would just be Mrs. So
and So. No thanks.

He married someone else and I married another.
For years we were apart but one night, almost
thirty years later, we ended up in the same place

again. He was still married to her and I was divorced from him. As if no time passed, we were together again until he died twenty years later. He never stopped being married to her. The house he purchased me was two streets over from theirs and we knew who the other was. She ignored me and I ignored her. When he died I didn't dress in black or attend his funeral, he had a wife for that.

In fact, I sat on my porch in a gold dress, the same color I wore when I first met him and watched the procession drive by. I knew she was in the limousine behind the hearse that carried his body. I was now in my seventies and had long ago stopped drinking beer or painting my lips red and could not bop or lindy hop any longer. In fact, the last five years of our time together was spent sitting and talking. The love was still there but all the fire that had once consumed us was banked. He was her husband but he was mine, first. That was how I felt.

~~YYYY~~

In her 84th year I sat talking to her and asked if she regretted her time spent with another woman's husband. She squinted at me in that way she had and didn't answer directly at first. She did ask me a question.

"Have you ever been a fool for a man?"

"Yes ma'am. But as soon as I realized I was being a fool I stopped." She nodded smiling.

"I know. We often talk about you. We are proud. But I didn't stop being a fool for him because I loved him and felt he was always mine even when he was married to her. He married her because he couldn't marry me. You see I could be his woman and accept the other women but I couldn't be his wife and accept it. That part didn't make sense to me. What I said probably doesn't make sense to you. But I'll say this, if I were twenty seven now I wouldn't settle for any of that; even if I met him first. You and a couple other young women taught this old hen that. Yes you did."

There is nothing quite like bought lessons and time…

5. *It Is My Turn… Damn the Rest*

Kenya was looking her future coldly in the eyes
and did not feel it had anything to do with the past
or the future. She was forty-five years of age and
the night before she celebrated graduating from
college as a Physician's Assistant, or what was
more widely known as a PA. It was her dream job.

*After graduating high school, she started college
and gotten a certification as a medical assistant.
Soon after graduating at nineteen she had gotten
pregnant and had a daughter who was now twenty-
five and working as a teacher. For the first ten
years of her daughter's life she worked hard and
took care of her daughter with irregular support
from a boyfriend she loved more than he loved her.
In fact, in the past ten years she had more than her
share of men she loved more than they loved her
but at twenty-nine she joined a church and made
the decision to find a man who loved her more. She*

knew it couldn't be the slick, handsome, street men
she was most attracted to but someone else.

She knew him as soon as she saw him. Feeling
eyes on her she looked up into the soft brown eyes
of a man who reminded her of Bryant Gumbel, the
former anchor who currently had his own sports
show on HBO. He was of regular height and size
and was good looking in an average way but had a
huge smile and he stared at her like she was a
goddess. She knew she was an attractive woman
with brown skin, a pretty smile and a much
slimmer figure than was currently fashionable but
she had something about her that men liked. She
smiled and he made his way to her. They engaged
in conversation and she discovered he worked as a
manager at one of the local shipping companies.
Like everything about him, he earned an average
salary. But he appealed to what she felt she needed
and for the next ten months they dated, he got to
know her daughter and he fell head over heels in

love with her and ten months to the day of their meeting they were married.

For almost fifteen years, they had their share of marital woes but they managed to make it through. He raised her daughter as his own and they also had a thirteen year old son together. He also supported her through her schooling and career advancement. By three years after marriage she was a registered nurse and now she was a PA and it was time for her. George was also no longer what interested her. During the last year of her studies and her residency, she met a man who was a PA and she was very attracted to him, and he to her. He was forty and had spent ten years in the military as a medic and had been a PA for the past five years. He was tall, dark, hard and handsome, all the things she once craved in a man. Jefferson to her personified man and not the acquiescent, too needy man she was married to.

Kenya knew George was behind her because he had always worn Drakkar cologne. He never did anything different. He was always the same salt of the earth man who lived by the rule books. She also knew if it hadn't been for her, they would still live in the same modest house, driving Honda Accords but they were now in a huge new home and she drove a Mercedes and he his dream truck. They were up to their eyeballs in debt but all appearances indicated they lived well.

Wrapping his arms around his wife's body, George kissed her neck. She stilled herself to keep from flinching. Pulling away, she turned to look at him. In her three-inch heels, she looked him directly in his eyes and she could see the love he felt for her clearly.

"I am so proud of you. Next step is doctor, I'm sure…" He said lovingly.

"I just want to enjoy this now George. Can you drop GII off at his karate practice and pick him up?"

GII, their son, was named for his father and looked like him but was lean and spare like his mother.

"I can but I thought you would. I am going in to work a couple of hours. My new assistant is doing well but needs a little more hands on."

"I was going to but I am meeting some people for an extended lunch and am not sure what time I will be done. The place is just past you." He realized in that moment she was dressed up in a swingy crepe dress and full makeup.

"I suppose so. You look really nice, it must be some meeting."

"It is. There are doctors and PAs and other professional types." She pecked him on the lips and hurried from the room, calling out to their son.

George felt trouble brewing in his gut. She was given to getting itchy every few years and this was that, he also felt she had been involved in more than one sexual fling during their marriage. It always started with her needing to get out and or flying in a rage about something and leaving.

"Dad…" George shook away his thoughts and turned to look at his son. He was growing up so fast and was a good kid. A bit of a nerd like him but spoiled like his mom.
"Seems, I will be taking you to soccer practice today, I can't stay but I will pick you up after. Maybe we can get lunch." GII's face opened in a huge smile.

"Cool… I have two classes today, so it will be three hours."

"That's good. That will give me time in the office."

"Do you think mom is coming back?" A chill ran up George's spine at his son's question.

"Of course she is; this is her home, here with us." He turned to get his things, not wanting his son to see the pain on his face.

He felt divided from Kenya. They hadn't made love in months and now this. He attributed it to her busyness but he just wasn't sure anymore. The party last night had been a good one and she seemed pleased by him throwing it. It was extravagant and over the top and he invited fifty friends and family. He was hoping that since she was done with school, and would be working three twelve hour days with four off, they would have more of a marital life and she would spend more time with GII.

"What are we going to do now?" Jefferson asked in his deep husky voice. For three hours he and Kenya enjoyed rich food and wine at a cozy restaurant off the beaten path, where no one knew them. When he invited her the night before he thought she would refuse. There had been intimate close encounters between them over the last few months, even a shared kiss but no alone time. He was feeling her and wanted her and he knew she was ripe for it because many nights in the cafeteria she shared her marriage woes with him. He wasn't interested in marrying her or in breaking up her marriage but was willing to do what her husband wasn't doing. He was also glad she found employment in another hospital.

"I'm game, don't you live near here?" He didn't say another word but snapped for the waiter and led her to his home.

She was all over him before they made it to his bedroom. Kenya was a ferociously sexual woman and was given to dominance. He didn't mind but also took the lead the second time to show her he wasn't that man.

YYYYY

Several hours after arriving home, George prepared food and sat down to dinner with his son. He was extremely concerned about Kenya. She had been gone for almost eight hours and he had not heard from her. He constantly checked his cell phone and even sent her two text messages that went unanswered.

When she finally arrived at nine, GII was asleep and George was waiting for her in the family room. She looked in at him, with a smile on her face. She held her shoes in her hand and he could tell she had been drinking. There was the relaxed look she got after imbibing. Normally, she looked tense and brittle.

"That most have been some soiree." George said.

"It was. There were lots of people and afterward a few of the girls and I went for drinks and banter. I had a great day. I am going to shower and go to bed." She waved, making her way up the stairs. He wanted to follow her and make her answer a few questions but he wasn't sure his heart could take the answers. An hour later he checked on Kenya and found her fast asleep, dressed in pajamas. Once he was in bed, he tried to wrap his arms around her but she swatted him away. Even in sleep she shunned him.

The next morning he asked her if she were attending church with him and GII and her answer was to pull the covers over her head. When they returned home, she was gone.

ΥΥΥΥΥ

For three months Kenya and George were passing ships. She worked more than forty hours in three days and slept away the next couple of days and on the other days off she would either pick up an extra shift or she was networking. It was rare that she had a meal with her husband and son, and she no longer attended church; that was her time, everything was about Kenya.

ΥΥΥΥΥ

Kenya was startled to wake up and find George sitting in the room with her. Glancing at the clock, she saw it was noon and she knew it was Monday, a day George normally worked.

"Is everything okay? Is GII okay?" she asked, sitting up.

"Does it matter Kenya?" George asked tiredly. Immediately her face tightened.

"What the hell does that mean? Of course it matters how my son is doing." She snapped.

"Considering you haven't seen him in months, I wouldn't know it matters."

Kicking the covers off, Kenya jumped out of bed. Her hair trigger temper had been unleashed. It was easy to make her angry when she was questioned and she was also prone to hitting him. That was why he often allowed things to go on.

"Don't start that soft shit George. I am building a damn career here. We have a lot to pay for." His eyes didn't waver from her. Her calling him soft used to insult him, now it just made him tired.

"You work three days a week Kenya and you sleep two. That leaves two other days you can choose to spend with your family but you choose to get more hours or whatever you are doing, what are you chasing Kenya?"

She swung to hit him but he caught her wrist. He had never responded to her hitting him but he felt there was something in her that wanted him to hit her. He felt he would then be more of a 'man' in her eyes. Since she couldn't hit him, she spat at him.

"I hate you George and I am sick of you and this damn marriage." She quickly raced into her personal bathroom and locked the door. He suddenly felt beaten. Within minutes she walked out fully dressed and left the house. He knew she had spoken the truth. He sat in his chair feeling raw and battle weary until it was time to pick up his son.

Arriving at the school, he was told his wife had taken his son out of school early. George got on the interstate and drove three hours, stopped for a meal and a walk before turning around and returning home.

He found Kenya pacing the floor when he arrived. Turning on him, she asked where he had been. Pushing past her, he walked upstairs to his son's room. For several minutes he watched GII with headphones on working on his homework on the computer and a half eaten McDonald's sandwich next to his. Walking over he lifted the headphones and kissed his son's face. GII turned in his chair to face his dad.

"Hey daddy, I'm sorry you and mom are getting divorced. I told her, I'm going to stay with you." George felt as if someone had punched him while simultaneously throwing scalding water in his face. He quickly sat down on the bed, to steady himself. He could not believe Kenya told their son that without consulting him.

"Son, your mom and I are having a hard time right now but I pray we can work it out. I don't want a divorce."

"Mom does, dad. She says she and you have outgrown this marriage. I know it doesn't mean you all do not love me." George felt sick inside. "It certainly doesn't mean that. We both love you son, more than anything. Why would you choose to stay with me, if there is...?"

"Dad, you are more patient with me and do more things and you are not as busy or as mad as mom. It is just us men together."

George's heart crumbled at his son's words. GII was a quiet studious kid but very astute, almost wise. Kenya, who was listening at the door, burst in her face distorted.

"I could make your little ass come with Me." she said to GII. Their son looked at his mother without blinking or flinching.

"No you cannot mom. I researched it and since I am over twelve, I get to decide and if you try to make me I will tell them you don't have time for me. You don't even know what's on my report card."

Twirling on her feet, Kenya raced from the room and out the house. George felt he needed to defend his wife.

"G don't disrespect your mom, she loves you."

"Dad, you taught me the truth is fair to everyone." He placed the headphones on his ears before picking up his sandwich and taking a bite. George touched his son's shoulder and made his way to his bedroom. Kenya didn't return home that night.

YYYYY

After sex, Kenya sat up in bed, looking down at Jefferson. He lay on his back, looking up at her.

"I'm leaving George." Her words made Jefferson sit up and pay closer attention.

"Why?" he asked, a perplexed look flitting across his face.

"It isn't working and why would I be in your bed if it was working?" she asked.

"I don't think of sex like that. Sex is one thing and marriage is something else. Leaving a marriage over sex seems stupid to me." Her brow lifted at his words.

"Could you clarify that, please?"

"My wife left me because I had sex outside our marriage. I would never have left her even though I had sex with other women. I loved her."

"So, you would have stayed if she stepped outside the marriage."

"Perhaps… I just don't think sex is the biggest or best thing marriage offers. Sex with just one person for the rest of your life is unnatural. If I ever marry again it won't be for that. But, I am certainly not considering marriage anytime soon. I wouldn't be hasty if I were you. I don't know your husband but he seems like a good dude. What about your son?"

She collapsed on the bed unable to believe Jefferson was saying what he was saying. She expected him to be happier to have more and open access to her.

"He is fine. He thinks his father is the man."

"That's a beautiful thing for a son to think." Jefferson said. Tired of talking, he started kissing his way down Kenya's body. He wasn't there for conversation.

It was three days before Kenya and George were in the same room again and that day she told him she was moving out. She had spoken to her mother, sisters and friends and only one had agreed with her. Her friend Paula, who had never been married nor had children, was in complete agreement. Everyone else told her she was a fool to let a good man go. They all watched George work to give her everything she asked of him and the thanks he got was her leaving at the pinnacle of their dreams being realized. Her mother was completely affronted.

"Kenya, you are saying that not only are you leaving your marriage but you are leaving your son? You are losing your mind." Kenya cussed profusely and stormed out.

YYYYY

"So just like that our marriage is over?" George asked as Kenya stood over him. She had given him her address and told him she found an apartment. And as usual she told GII before talking to her husband. George felt as if life were draining from him. He loved her so much and would forgive her anything if she would not leave.

"George, we have been ending for years… we just held on…"

"Until you got your degree and certification?" he asked drily. She felt enraged by the truth of his words and kicked his chair.

"I don't know what you are accusing me of but I deserve happiness and I am not happy."

"Kenya what you think makes you happy constantly changes, first it was a bigger house, then a fancier car, then becoming a PA, now I am sure it is some street guy filling you up with words... what next Kenya?"

She was unable to respond. His words felt like arrows to her ego but she wasn't going to change her mind.

"You are willing to devastate our family to be happy... a happy that is endless and changing." George said not without rancor. She swung at him and he grabbed her wrist, pushing her away roughly. She landed on her tailbone and sat on the floor stunned.

"Sometimes you push too hard Kenya. Let that be the last time you grab me."

YYYYY

For almost a year, George chased Kenya, begging her to return, even calling friends and family asking them to intervene on his family's behalf. However, Kenya was adamant in her desire to be free and filed for divorce asking to see her son two nights a week and half the proceeds from selling of the house. Neither could afford it without the other.

George was debilitated for months and continually prayed for his wife to return. Eventually, he stopped praying for that and simply asked God to do what was his will.

Jefferson dropped off the scene shortly after Kenya moved out, making it clear he wasn't interested in being her only man. Since him there had been a few of the same type. She thought she was having a good time but there were too many nights when she felt lost and unsure but was unable to admit it.

Almost eighteen months after moving out and six months after the divorce she faced her feelings. A friend convinced her to attend a banquet for black professionals. It was an annual event that donated money for scholarships for African American youth. Walking in, she was stunned to see George in a blue tuxedo, twenty pounds lighter and with a woman who appeared to be in her mid-thirties. She hadn't seen or spoken to George since the divorce became final six months earlier. She picked GII up after school when he stayed over and dropped him off at George's new, much smaller home without getting out of the car. Her friend, Samantha nudged her, leading her to their table.

"George looks great doesn't he?" Samantha asked after they were seated and gotten wine.
"Umm, I didn't know he was dating."

"Why would you?" Samantha asked and looked around. The program started but Kenya remained focused on George and his date. During the meet and mingle period, she made her way to them. "He is no longer your husband." She thought but continued her trek.

"Hello George." She said. Turning to her, he had a genuine smile on his face. He looked at her as he would a friend he once was close to.

"Hi Kenya, this is Dr. Mariana Lester, she is the new director of the Virtual School. Mariana, this is my ex-wife Kenya." Mariana offered her hand, which Kenya ignored.

"Where is GII?" Kenya asked.

"He is home. Our son is fifteen and quite capable of being alone a few hours. Please excuse me."

Taking Mariana by the elbow, he led her away. Kenya wanted to throw something or scream. What she was going to do was leave.

ΥΥΥΥΥ

GII was surprised to see his mother on the doorstep.

"Hey mom, are you okay?" GII asked as Kenya stepped inside, looking around. She noted house was furnished with the furniture from their former home. Her eyes filled with tears because unlike her, George held on to things that were theirs. Everything she currently owned was hers.

"I am. I just saw your dad and wanted to check on you. How often are you alone?"

"Rarely, but I am capable and dad knows he can trust me." He said.

Kenya plopped down on the sage leather couch she purchased three years earlier. Warily, GII sat across from his mom. The time he spent with Kenya usually involved eating out and a movie occasionally. They didn't discuss much.

"So, your dad is dating." GII kept his face blank.

"Mom, I don't discuss that stuff with you about dad because you two are divorced." Kenya looked at her son and no longer saw a boy but a man. He was taller than her and George, and, she noted with a hint of sadness, he had a light mustache.

"True. Would you like to get some food or something or go somewhere?" she asked hopefully. He had homework but could see something he had never seen on his mom's face. Yearning.

"Sure let me text dad and we can go somewhere."

During dinner she asked questions about school and even girls but dropped him off at home feeling it was too little too late. Her son had developed a full life without her. He loved her but she was not part of his day-to-day life. She had never been.

ΥΥΥΥΥ

I knew of Kenya for years, we were in and out of the same circles in various ways. I was ten years older and we were by no means friends but she often showed up at events where I spoke. After one such event I was sitting in a large room, sipping tea, relaxing and she walked in. She was almost fifty, over four years post-divorce and her son was in his first year of college in California. She pulled up a chair and sat near me.

"Your topic on marriage was interesting and enlightening." Smiling tiredly, I asked her what she meant. I really wanted to be alone with my tea and thoughts. The day had drained me and I regrouped quietly and alone but I could sense she needed something and ministry didn't rest.

"What specifically?" I asked.

"The parts on marriage like life is full of seasons and every woman including you, have those moments when they think of greener grass but grown women know that grass turns brown in fall and can die in the winter but come spring and fall, there is newness."

"I believe that. There have been many times in almost four decades of marriage when I wanted to pack my bags and go to Maine or somewhere. Times when everything my husband said or did was an annoyance to me and who I felt I was.

However, I was always a big picture woman and even in those moments I never stopped loving him or felt he didn't love me. There are those who can live without loving or being loved. I am not that woman. Thus, as long as I loved and am loved, there is no mature or real reason to go."

"I left because I never felt I loved my husband enough, though I always knew he loved me. I thought he was weak because he catered to me and I wanted strong or what looked like strong. Even the way he made love to me, so soft, loving and lavishing bothered me. I was a fool. Do you know when I realized I really loved him?"

I shrugged. She came to talk and she needed someone, anyone to listen.

"About three years ago when I saw him with another woman, I realized what I lost. She was attentive and his eyes looked upon her in much the way they once looked upon me. I hurt and harmed him and he survived to love again. I will admit that after that day I tried to wiggle my way in, I thought to take him from her but really it was because too late, I realized how much I loved him and how much I lost. I have everything I thought I wanted, I earn lots of money, live in a nice home and drive the best car etc., yet I don't have anything really. At my age men will still sleep with me but love me…"

"Perhaps you are still looking in all the wrong places. According to you, you had a great man who is no longer available but I suspect you are not looking for men like him still…"

For several minutes she stared at me and didn't say a word but I saw a range of emotions flicker across her face. She stood and looked down at me.

"You could be right. Thanks." She walked out and left me to my tea. I said a small prayer for her that at some point she would just be still and allow love to find her, because searching with the same tools rarely worked.

6. *I Still Look Good... Mama Used to Say...*

Staring in the mirror, Andrea knew she looked good at forty-five. She was fit, her hair and makeup were on point, and she dressed well. Then why in the hell wasn't she getting asked out or when she was out why did men pass her over as if they didn't see her for a woman who clearly didn't look as good. From the time she was sixteen and learned how to do her hair and skillfully apply makeup, not to mention developing a sexy body, men had been at her beck and call, handsome men, paid men, even a few famous men. Now all of a sudden it was as if she didn't exist. She had been in a long-term relationship from age thirty-nine until recently and that had ended. Andrea was sure that once she was back on the market the men would all pause... when she walked into the room. That had not happened. She shared back to the first time she knew the men wanted her and to the previous night when she felt they no longer did...

"On my sixteenth birthday, I was at my first dance. That day I prepared as if for the prom. I got my hair done, makeup professionally applied, I also got skintight jeans and a shirt that draped some areas and hugged others. I was what they called fine. My breasts were high and full, my butt was the same and I had a slim waist and tight thighs. Men and boys had been looking at me the past year since I filled out but I hadn't had a chance to get out of the house and now I was free. When I walked into the party it was as if time stopped. They guys all turned to look at me and I flounced my hair, smiling. I danced all night and never felt more beautiful.

At the end of the night Terrell Favors walked up to with a huge smile on his face. I felt my heart race. Terrell was twenty-one and just signed with a professional basketball team. He had always been a heartthrob but having just signed a contract

109

worth several hundred thousand dollars annually really made women hearts and other parts throb and he was smiling at me. Tossing back my hair, I looked up at him.

"Hey beautiful, you must be new around here?"

"I am new tonight but I have been here, just sitting inside growing up." He chuckled at my audacity and asked me to go outside with him. The dance was being held near a pond and we walked down near it and sat on a bench.

"I'm in town for the summer and I would love to spend some time with you. How old are you?"

"Old enough I said."

That night we didn't do much but kiss and touch but I was ready for what he offered. For the next several weeks I lied to mama about my work hours and Terrell picked me up and we went to his hotel where he introduced me to sex. It really wasn't that great because it was over so quickly but mostly he wanted me to perform oral sex and I was willing to learn and do anything to please him, after all he was Terrell Favors. Something that solidified what we were doing and my future in many ways was he always gave me gifts of moderately priced jewelry and cash. He was very discreet and usually handed me a gift bag with nice gold earrings, a bracelet or something and there was usually a few hundred dollars inside. At the end of the summer he told me he would keep in touch but of course he didn't. After that I only saw him on television playing ball and two years later when he married the girl he dated since high school. However, Terrell had unleashed my desire for male attention, gifts and money."

For the next three years through high school and beauty school, Andrea had her share of men who

111

added to her bottom line. Some were like Terrell and were mediocre sexually, others were better at sex and other things. A time or two she fancied herself in love but the guys had other ideas.

By the time she was in her thirties that was her life until she fell in love with a man and was with him exclusively for almost six years. By then she had a successful hair salon and a boyfriend she hoped would become a husband but several months earlier he walked away from his job, the city and her, leaving her, for the first time in a long time, back on the market at forty-five.

Then the previous night happened…

After a long day in the salon, she dressed to impress and made her way to Jazz Hop, a club known for the best in jazz and hip-hop and was becoming known for catering to the over thirty-five set. She felt good and knew she looked good, walking in. Taking a seat at the bar, she ordered red wine and looked around. There were many seemingly unattached men who were well-dressed and conversing amongst themselves. She smiled, sipping from her glass, noticing the other women. She saw and sensed a bohemian, eclectic vibe from the women and noted most of them had natural hairdos. She also noticed they didn't look as if they were trying to get attention but they were getting it. Several of the men flocked to them, engaging in conversation and laughter. She watched until she felt someone walk up next to her and she turned to face him. He was an attractive man who looked to be her age with close-cropped hair and a beard and mustache with sprinkles of silver. He was tall and fit with milk chocolate skin.

"Are you new here?" He asked in a deep cultured tone.

"I am new to this club but I live in the city and you?"

"I am an old head around here. My brother and I opened it a couple years ago, he is about hip-hop with an adult vibe and jazz is my thing, I fancy myself a bit of a jazzman. I worked for IBM for twenty-five years and I retired to do this."

"What is this exactly?" She asked. His eyes never wavered from hers.

"This is a place filled with music, food and conversation for those of like minds who aren't about the pickup, or trying to find someone but just to engage and create friendships." There was something about his message that felt pointed.

She suddenly felt underdressed in her snug knit dress that showed her curvaceous body and stopped inches above her knees. She had to still herself not to tug her hem. Her eyes flitted around and she noticed most of the women wore either jeans or baggy dresses of midi or maxi length. Most also wore little to no makeup.

"Excalibur is a nice place also, it caters to a more diverse clientele and there are a lot of older brothers there." His words felt as if he had thrown a drink in her face.

"Older brothers, how old are you sir?"

"I'm forty seven and I know you aren't my age yet and you are beautiful…"

"But not what your crowd accepts or embraces… I am too old, not organic enough or whatever the word is these days. Also, my hair isn't natural nor is the fabric of my dress." She said, trying to keep her voice light.

"I didn't say any of that. As a proprietor, it is my business to assess my crowd and have them feel comfortable. My apologies if I offended you." He said, his intense gaze not leaving hers.

Turning on the plush barstool, she slowly sipped her wine. She refused to get up and leave quickly. For two hours, she enjoyed the music and another glass of excellent wine and heard the laughter and repartee around her. Not one other person made their way to her to engage or even make eye contact.

After leaving the club she stood on the sidewalk allowing the cool air to caress her bare shoulders. She had never felt as alone in her life. Her mom, Mabel Livingston raised her and her sisters to always look good, find a man who would take care of them but to ultimately only depend on themselves. Mabel had given birth to three girls in six years from three different men and never worked a day in her life, not on the books as she called it. Mabel was an extraordinary hair stylist and to this day she 'did hair' as she called it in a screened porch off her kitchen. Most of her clients were older women who got their hair straightened and curled. Mabel owned a modest home she paid for by doing hair and the men in her life and at sixty-five still was a sexy always well-dressed woman. She was Andrea's model for life and suddenly she felt the model failed as she stood looking at herself. She needed to see her mom.

~~YYYYY~~

Assessing her mother as she sat on the porch next to her, Andrea smiled at Mabel's shoulder length and shiny auburn hair. Her face was also expertly made up. She was wearing a dress with two-inch heeled sandals and her nails both finger and toe were fire engine red. She looked content sipping her tea.

Mabel also checked her daughter out, with her hair and nails done with muted makeup and dressed in designer jeans. She also noticed Andrea looked sad. Andrea was the youngest of her three daughters, Alicia was forty-eight and Anja forty-six, neither of her girls were married but they all had good lives, she felt. Alicia had two children and like Andrea, Anja didn't have any. They were all lovely girls. The two older ones were living and working in Atlanta, all in the beauty business like their mother but Andrea was the most successful with her own salon and lots of clients.

"Did you ever want more Mom?" Andrea asked.

"More than what baby?"

"More than doing hair, having a man or two who helped pay the bills or this?" Andrea asked, waving her hand around the porch.

"Not really, I have it way better than my people did. Mama had seven of us, and daddy drank up what money he earned, so mama made do. They never owned a home or anything. The best years of Mama's life was when daddy died and she lived here with me, getting his social security after he died which means she had ten good years and died at eighty-three. On the other hand, I lived my life, had my girls and the three of you never needed for anything and didn't want for much. Between y'all daddies, my other men, and my straightening comb, we had. You and your sisters all take care of yourselves and don't ask anyone for anything. That's a good life to me. Nowadays, I do hair when I want to. I got a little savings and that, with my SSI, is all I need. Don't want much else." Mabel said.

"Did you ever want a husband?"

"I had two or three but they weren't mine." Mabel said with humor. Andrea cringed at her words because she remembered when Mabel was seeing one of her friend's fathers and she was always worried it would be discovered. "Is that why you're looking all long in the mouth because that boy up and left here and never married you?"

Andrea blinked back tears at her mom's insight.

"Baby, the minute you let him move in, the likelihood of him marrying you was over. He sucked up what you offered and then he was gone to probably the next one."

"But mom he contributed and did things for me, it wasn't as if he was leeching off me."

"Umm hmm but a man is still a man and as much as women have changed some men stay the same... there are the women they live with and or

120

have sex with and there are those they marry. He was also younger than you. He might have started to think about making babies."

Mabel's words felt painful and tasted like iron in Andrea's mouth. She told her about the club incident.

"Andrea, that man did you a favor. I see these nappy headed girls running around here with those dreadful locks and hairdos, some even have hair under their arms. That is all a passing thing; good looking women never go out of style."

"Mom, you might want to look closer, some of those girls are stunning in their naturalness and men, real men seem to love that."

Turning up her nose, Mabel stared at her daughter.

"I don't need to look closer at anything. I have seen fads come and go. I grew up in the sixties and I never stopped straightening my hair or painting my lips and never once did I go lacking for a man. However, I knew my market and that is where I shopped. It seems to me like you are a Publix supermarket woman who goes shopping at Whole Foods."

Andrea had to chuckle at her mom's words and how clearly she saw things.

"I hear you mom but I have been that chick for so long, I guess I miss walking in a room and having men stop and look. When I was with Marcus, I didn't care if men noticed me or not, I had a man but now I do care. I'm lonely and I'm not looking for a husband, necessarily but I want a man in my life. A good and caring man, he doesn't have to do anything other than that. I can pay all my own bills and have money left over."

"Like I said, you are shopping the wrong aisles. You are not jazz and rap music or poetry. You are soulful music baby: backyard barbecues and men who can appreciate a grown woman and what she brings. You can continue casting your pole in the wrong pond and you will likely grow old and angry and that doesn't look good on anyone."

Andrea heard and understood what her mom was trying to say. She was thirty-eight to Marcus' thirty-two when they got together, he had been jazz, and hip-hop and being with him convinced her she was also. But like her mom said, all the men who had been there for her and wanted what she offered had been soul music and barbecue. Perhaps, she was eating the wrong food and listening to the wrong music. She had to bring who she was to an audience with an appreciation for it and her...

Mabel always knew...

7. *I Loved Men Before I Changed…*

Lena walked into the room with authority. Some would say she looked butch dressed in jeans, a t-shirt and boots with short cut hair and small piercings in her ears but there was something decidedly feminine about her face which was free of makeup. Her skin was sienna colored with brown eyes, pure brown, with the longest lashes, a nose that flared and perfect lips that looked tinted with light rose but they were her natural color. She was fifty-four, the mother of two grown daughters and had been divorced four years earlier after having an affair with a woman. Her story intrigued me because, for the most part, I felt people were hetero or homosexual with some shades of bisexuality. But Lena clearly defined herself as a heterosexual woman, satisfied with her sex life before the change… after the change she refused to define herself, just be herself…

She shook my hand firmly and sat before me, her eyes holding mine. I had so many questions but I would start with the one intriguing me most.

"What do you consider the change?"

"It was two things, I was literally going through what our ancestors called the change which was menopause and I met a woman who appealed to me on so many levels including sexually."

"So prior to that you weren't attracted to women?"

"I have always been attracted to women as people. I was close to my mom, my aunts and am very close to my daughters who are thirty and thirty-three. I got married at twenty-one and had a baby nine months later and one three years after that and I adored those little people. And before you ask, I had great sex with my husband which included orgasms. He was my best friend and lover."

I jotted down a few notes, trying to get my mind right for the other questions. I genuinely wanted to know but didn't want to offend her, though my instincts told me she would be hard to offend. There was something comfortable and serene about her.

"How did you meet your husband?"

"As you know I am an artist, however when I completed college with a degree in Art my only option was to teach. Instead, I took a job as a welder, which not only allowed me to be somewhat artistic it also allowed me to make twice as much as teachers. My ex Aaron was my supervisor. I was immediately attracted to him and we became friends and lovers and married. We had a great marriage though I hurt him badly at the end."

"How did you tell him?"

"I met a woman who was in one of my sculpture classes and she wowed me. Not just with her looks which were very femme but edgy. It was how she did things. Her art was as if she made love to it and she ate with relish in the same way and laughed and danced from somewhere in her core. In my classes we do all things artistic such as dancing and cooking etc. It isn't just sculpture and painting. My feelings for her scared me so I avoided being alone with her. She was always in my head when I wasn't around her and being around her was almost too much. One night it started raining, and all my students hurried out, leaving on her and myself. She told me she didn't have a ride and I told her I would drive her after I cleaned up."

Lena stopped speaking and it was clear from her heightened color she was reminiscing.

"She turned on the music in the other room; it was sultry Indian music that we often played in class. When I walked in to tell her I was ready I got the shock of my life. She was naked and dancing in the middle of the floor completely free. Her eyes were closed and her movements were perfectly in sync with the music. I had never seen anything more beautiful and I was unable to move. She opened her eyes and continued dancing, making her way to me. She walked into my arms and kissed me and I was lost to her."

For weeks, I was with her in the studio until early morning hours and at home I could barely face my husband. The girls were already gone. He went to work at six and I usually got in about one or two, which wasn't that unusual because I got lost in my work after class hours. But he knew me and sensed a change in me and knew something was awry. We were connected. He asked if I were having an affair and I confessed I was, with a woman. I could see a light go out in his eyes. I would love to tell you he understood but he didn't. He's human, and he yelled at me and rushed out to keep from slapping me, I'm sure.

We had been married almost twenty-nine years and I was telling him what we had, I gave to someone else. He called the girls and told them and he never returned to the home we shared. I reached out but he was unable to talk to me. It has been over four years and we are cordial when we see each other. We never again discussed my duplicity. He filed for divorce immediately. He has remarried."

"How did your daughters take it?"

"Surprisingly well, they wanted me and their dad happy. My oldest did ask a lot of questions such as why I waited so long to be a lesbian. I answered as best I could. My heart was broken because I broke his. My youngest daughter is one of those people who had always said and believed sexuality was fluid. They didn't like that I hurt their daddy but they love their mom."

I felt her words and was glad for her that her children didn't shun her.

"How long did your relationship last with that first woman." Delighted laughter flew from Lena's throat.

"It wasn't a relationship and it was over pretty much as soon as my husband left. I stopped teaching for a few months and traveled around the world a bit. I was now single and wanted adventures. I went to the Caribbean, Thailand, and Alaska, one trip behind the other. She was an adventure as well, I suppose. I enjoyed it and her immensely."

"Did anyone aggressively disapprove?"

"Oh yes, my parents and my husband's mother were horrified. My dad was more embarrassed than anything, and my mom felt she had failed me somehow. They didn't disown me or anything like that, but at the time they were in their seventies and could not understand their fifty-year-old daughter changing like that. Mom questioned me until she exhausted us both but dad never talked about it again. I see them at least twice a month for meals. We don't discuss my personal life and we focus on what affects all of us. However, my ex's mom called me dykes and everything she could think of. She no longer speaks to me. I understand, I really do, and I regret all the pain I caused all of them. She tried to get my ex to get me to give him money for the house. We had fixed the house up together but it was a house I was purchasing when he married me and I guess he didn't want to do that."

"Did you ever have sex with a man again?"

Lena smiled as if she were waiting for that question.

"I have not, but I see men who I find attractive. Men rarely approach me but women do. I have had several flings and am now in a relationship that has gone on for a year. She is forty and has never been sexually involved with a man. She calls herself a real lesbian." Lena grinned, showing perfect teeth.

"Did you always dress and look as you do now?"

"Pretty much, my hair was longer during my marriage because my husband loved my soft hair but I never wore makeup and always dressed in jeans, boots and shirts. That is who I am."

"Do you think menopause changed your desires?"

"I don't know. I do know that I was going through both changes at the same time. I don't evaluate myself that deeply. I have gotten over the guilt of hurting people. My ex is happily married and my girls have great lives as do my parents. Now, I am living, loving, and enjoying my life."

"Would you do anything differently, if you could?"

"Not one thing. I loved him and honored what we had for almost thirty years, I loved and raised good kids and respected and loved my parents. All of those things bought me to this whole place I am living in now. I enjoy women and all they bring to life, including sex with them. And since you didn't ask, no I'm not worrying God will strike me dead either, which is something I'm sure my ex mother-in-law prayed for."

More laughter poured from her and I realized she was happy with the changes that occurred in her life and was open and honest as could be about how she was living.

8. But... I AM A DARLING

"How is this possible?" Debra thought as she sat at the function alone.

She thought for sure someone would ask her out and be there with her. It had been a year since Wallace passed and she was back on the market and ready for love. She had not gotten married until she was forty-seven and Wallace was ten years older. When she met him she was immediately swept off her feet. Wallace was handsome, immaculately dressed, and drove a Jaguar. She had never in her life seen the inside of a Jaguar not to mention riding in one.

Debra left home at nineteen to find fame and fortune in New York. Her parents had tried to dissuade her but she was determined. She knew she could be a star. She was talented, could dance and sing and she was stunning. She had been told that all of her life. She was average height with curves galore but what made men swoon was her fine pale skin, that was the color of the lightest brown egg and her naturally red hair that was long and almost straight. Everyone from her parents to friends and family had always been enamoured with her for those reasons and treated her accordingly. She was the youngest of three sisters, all of whom were closer to the complexion of her mother, a rich pecan. She had taken on the skin tone and hair color of her paternal relatives and the tendency to be a darling. A darling was a woman who was treated and felt special because of the way she looked and it almost always, in Alabama, consisted of light skin and abundant hair. Debra's parents had catered to her and she was never expected to do chores or anything her much older sisters had done. Her parents were in their forties when she was born and her sisters sixteen and nineteen. They all doted on her. She was their darling and she expected that from the world.

New York didn't work out as she hoped. Arriving there she quickly discovered there were many darlings in the world and many were more talented, beautiful or something. To support herself she got a job as a typist at the phone company for several years until she gave up and moved to Jacksonville, Florida. There she snagged a job as secretary for an attorney she had an affair with, and for more than twenty-five years she worked, took care of herself and had a series of affairs in between being the lead singer at a local church. Singing in the choir was her claim to the fame she sought and it was how she met Wallace. He was a visiting pastor who recently lost his wife and had two grown daughters living in Seattle, Washington. He was also a business owner who made a good deal of money as a contractor for the federal government from where he recently retired.

As she stood singing, she could feel his eyes on her and she amped it up a bit. She was forty-seven and looking for love, a love she could call her own.

Walking out the church after the service, Debra saw Wallace standing near his car. When he spotted her, he made his way to her.

"Good morning chanteuse, your beautiful voice made my morning." Batting her lashes and pulling her shawl closer to her, Debra smiled slightly.

"Well, you should have been listening to Pastor." She purred.

"Pastor wasn't speaking when you were singing." He responded. "I am a Pastor in remission, Wallace Sanders and you are?"

"I am Debra, Debra Anders. Why are you in remission?"

"I will tell you all about it if you join me for lunch. I have standing reservations at Capital Grille."

She was impressed by the restaurant and most Sundays her dinner consisted of a local cafeteria. She didn't have money for fancy restaurants. Her eyes raked over him, taking in his suit, shiny shoes and back to his handsome face adorned with a thin mustache. He looked good enough for lunch.

"What about my car?" she asked.

"I will follow you home and then drive us to lunch." Nodding in acceptance she made her way to her car.

Wallace followed her to a nice, small apartment complex where the patrons parked in front of their places. All of the apartments were two bedrooms with a patio and on one level. There was also a community center and pool area. To Wallace it looked more like a retirement complex rather than the place for a vibrant woman like Debra.

Once she was in his car, she sunk into the plush seats. He didn't say much on the drive to the restaurant but the sounds of Bebe Winans filled the car. Wallace allowed the valet to park the car and he escorted Debra inside. The host recognized Wallace and led them to an excellent table that was a bit secluded. Debra felt slightly overwhelmed.

"You must be a VIP or something." She said.

"Not at all, I am simply a widower who can't cook and loves good food. This is near the home I purchased."

"Oh, you live near here. This is a pretty exclusive area. And I am sorry to hear about your wife. How long ago did she pass?"

"Six months but she was sick a long time. You are so beautiful." He said and she blushed furiously, glancing at the menu. The waiter arrived and she quickly ordered French onion soup and grilled salmon. Wallace ordered chowder and the dry aged rib eye.

"Tell me about yourself Debra."

"I'm a legal secretary, I was born in Mobile, Alabama, lived in New York a few years and have been here twenty-five years. For those years, I have worked for the same law firm as a secretary. I have two older sisters and my mother in Mobile. My father died ten years ago."

"Why did you leave New York, you look like a New York kind of woman." She snorted, delicately.

"That's what I thought too but I didn't sing or dance well enough and after so many rejections I worked a few years and then moved here. I am able to clothe and provide for myself."

"No husband or children."

"Not a one." She said and he heard wistfulness in her voice.

"Why?" she tried to think of something but simply told the truth instead.

"I didn't date marriageable men and a kid wasn't an option unless I was married. Time passes very quickly."

"It does. I was married thirty-five years. I got married at twenty-two and my wife was twenty. We grew up together. I went to college and married her a year after graduation. We have two daughters, thirty-four and thirty. They are both school teachers in Seattle. Like you, neither is married but I keep hoping."

"I am sure it is because you want grandchildren." He grinned at her charmingly and the waiter arrived with their food.

After dinner they drove to the beach and sat in the car with jazz music playing.

"Wallace, I am celibate. I have been for three years. For years I played with God by being in men's beds and then getting up and going to church."

"No problem..." was his answer.

It took three months of wining and dining for Wallace to propose and Debra to accept. He was everything she wanted in a husband. He had a beautiful home, a nice car and an excellent income coming in monthly. Wallace on the other hand was head over heels enamoured with Debra. She felt for lack of a better word like his trophy wife. The only wrinkle was both his daughters felt he was marrying too soon after the death of their mother and refused to bless the marriage or attend the wedding. Debra was unconcerned because Wallace didn't seem to be. He made it clear he loved her.

YYYYY

Marriage to Wallace was everything Debra prayed it was and hoped it wasn't. He was loving, attentive and good in bed. He also catered to her wants and needs, immediately upgrading her car and lifestyle and telling her she didn't have to work. She was his darling.

What she hadn't anticipated was Wallace's expectations of her as a wife. He wanted home cooked meals at least four days a week and he felt she didn't need the amount of time with her church friends as she once had. She did the best she could but always felt she fell short on those things. It was hard to step from being on her own for almost fifty years and never preparing a meal other than breakfast into being a full time homemaker. She once told him her parents had never expected her to cook, clean, or do chores. She remembered his words...

"I am not your parents, I am your husband and I'm doing my part and I have expectations of you doing your part. That's how marriage and partnerships work." His voice was low and deep and she felt his words deep in her soul. He loved and pampered her but he had expectations. She had thought that as long as she looked good and was available in bed, their lives would consist of dinners at fancy restaurants and a maid to clean. She would spend her days leisurely or with friends and her evenings and nights with him. Because she didn't want to lose what she had, she learned to adapt.

His daughters never came completely around but they were well-raised women and once a year they both came to visit for a week and they spent those times seeing sites, dinners out and attending church services on Sunday before departing.

Wallace and Debra were in a good groove when on his sixty-seventh birthday Wallace collapsed on the golf course and died of a massive heart attack.

For the next several weeks Debra was in a fog and allowed her friends and Wallace's daughters to handle everything. She couldn't believe the man she took for granted but who she loved more than she realized was gone. The day before he died they were making plans for travelling more and then he was gone.

For months Debra visited her family and friends around the country and attended conferences, anything not to be alone. Wallace had left her enough in insurance money to live on comfortably and she didn't have a house payment. She had the usual monthly expenses and a car payment. He had done well by her even in his death but after a year of flitting from here to there, she was lonely and wanted companionship. What she really wanted was a husband, another man just like Wallace.

~~YYYYY~~

Debra and I met at church; we served together and were friendly. We had not done many things together but one day she approached me and asked if I wanted to go to lunch after church and I accepted. My husband had a meeting that involved food and I didn't want to eat alone.

"How are you?" I asked after we were seated and served at the restaurant.

"I'm good. It has been a year of mixed feelings and emotions. I am ready to marry again but it seems I am no longer... it just isn't working."

I felt a tug on my heart at her words and I really wanted her to tell me what was on her mind. I felt that was why she asked me out.

"What were you going to say?"

"I was going to say, I no longer seem to have the appeal I once did. Men seem to look right through me."

I understood her words and I actually understood more than she was saying. When I met her fifteen years earlier she had been in her early forties and a very striking woman, slender but shapely with long naturally red hair and pale skin that drew attraction based on those attributes alone. I had often watched her as men watched her and they almost fell out of their seats to assist her in some ways. Even after she married, it was like that initially. However, she was now in her later fifties and considerably heavier, her red hair looked too red, and there was more than a few lines in her face. She was an attractive woman but the honest to God's truth she was an older attractive woman who would never generate the same kind of attraction. That was simply how that all worked out. I noticed she was doing the same kind of preening and posturing she had done fifteen years earlier and it didn't have the same kind of effect.

"It is often that way I suspect after one is married for a long time." I said carefully. Her light eyes found mine and I could see the sadness and a bit of fear.

"Do you think it is because men think I will compare them to Wallace?" She asked.

"That is part of it but the other part is you have a brand new car and live in a fabulous home and there are men who will be intimidated by that. Also, you have to be very cautious of those who will only want to date you because you have those things. There are lots of men who want a sugar mama." I said, trying to add humor to a rather heavy conversation.

That was one of those days when I wished people didn't seek me out for advice because there were times when I knew they simply didn't want to hear home truths. I also knew I had to be honest with as much compassion as possible. I was seven years younger and just turned fifty and felt her pain.

"I know about the predators. I have met more than my share of those lately. Either they want to jump in bed or they look at me like they want me to take care of them. No thanks on that but I want a man who will treat me and take care of me like Wallace did, I won't settle for less. When I met him I was barely making my ends meet, had never owned a home or a new car and he lavished me with all of that." Her voice was strong and adamant. I was quiet for several minutes, focusing on sweetening my tea.

"Say something!" she said.

Stopping what I was doing, I looked up at her. I knew I had to be as real and raw with her as I was with the young women I tutored and mentored.

"Debra, you are a beautiful woman who loves God and has a lot to offer but there are cold hard facts. The first being is that every day in this country more men die earlier than women which means the market is filled with eligible women, who these days have lots going on for themselves. You have a beautiful home, a new car and your hands, ears and wrists have nice jewelry. It might not be that many men who can live up to the standard Wallace set." She rolled her eyes but that didn't deter me, she had come to me for a reason. "Not only that but most of the men I see in their late fifties and older who have resources and are widowed or divorced or are going for what is currently called trophy wives..."

"Are you saying I can't be a man's trophy?" she snapped.

"No indeed, I am not. What I am saying is those who are traditionally viewed as trophies are usually between the ages of thirty and fifty. They aren't embarrassingly young for those men but they are much younger than the men they marry. In my marriage classes, I get young couples and then there are those where the husband is usually twenty years older or more. Many of the women in their thirties are marrying men in their fifties who are well to do and willing to give them a baby. For the women in their forties and fifties they are getting the same guys except in these cases all the baby-making is over but they are with women they can feel younger with."

Debra's eyes filled with tears that threatened to spill over.

"So, at almost fifty-eight I'm washed up and either have to find a man in his eighties or not get married at all."

"Debra, I'm not saying that at all. What I'm doing is telling you what the real deal is. That is why we see so many sisters our age doing things such as travel, etc., with other women. There is a new market and that is the younger man. However, that not wanting to have sex until married thing might be a deal breaker; even the brothers in church want to sample the goodies."

"Are you kidding? I have gained thirty pounds in ten years and most of it is hanging slack on my body. There is no way I'm getting naked in front of some young man. Younger men never really paid me much attention anyway. I was never their type; they always went for your type." My brow arched, waiting for her to expound on that.

"You are fifty and look forty-three and you have that sister shape, with a big high butt and standup boobs, my butt is as flat as a flounder and boobs sagged when I was in high school. The men I dated didn't mind that, they just wanted to be with a woman who looked like me."

She wasn't going to say it, but I was. We were going for broke and if this was the last lunch...

"By that you mean really light-skinned women. Were most of your exes' dark skinned men?" Her face flushed.

"They all were. Many said things about my skin tone against theirs, ignoring the sagging boobs and flat butt. Wallace never said it but it was always the beige elephant in the room. His first wife was dark like him." Her voice trembled.

"I am ashamed to say that was my calling card. My parents even treated me better than my older sisters because of it. My daddy was light but not as light as me but his family was. My sisters and my mom are pecan colored. My sisters are sixteen and nineteen years older than me. I always felt that's why Wallace's daughters didn't like me. I was so different than his ex-wife in complexion and temperament. I do not feel old."

"And you aren't. Life is just beginning these days at your age. But since you are no longer a darling, you will have to mix and mingle and not wait for men to drop at your feet."

"What is a darling?"

"A woman who expects to be catered to for the whole of her life, mostly by men. The darling age has passed."

For the first time since we got together, she actually laughed out loud and relaxed a bit.

"You are too honest but I appreciate you. I have one more question. Is my hair too red?"

"Entirely. You would look beautiful with a cocoa color and a shorter cut. Also go where men are, such as golf courses, walk the tracks at the high school and those kinds of places. Pastor also has a senior singles ministry, sign up for that." She batted her lashes and didn't respond but I knew she felt and heard what I was saying and I prayed she knew it came from a place of love.

¥¥¥¥¥

For three months I didn't see her. I went on vacation and we attended different services but when we had our next class, she sashayed in and sat at my table. She looked like a different woman.

Her hair was cut shorter and was sassy and swingy. It was also in a flattering bronze color. She also seemed trimmer in her white capris and bright green t-shirt.

"You look fabulous Debra."

"Thanks. You taught me it's never too late to change a bit. I started taking a seniors golf class and met the instructor. He is in his early seventies and quite fit and handsome. He is long divorced with no children. Thank God for the no children. He wants us to travel to Mexico in two weeks but I told him I would need a separate room. I don't give away my goodies to men I'm not married to."

Reaching over, I slapped her palm.

"Also, I had a tummy tuck and it is still healing." Laughter poured from my throat at her words.

A true darling was always a darling... I was not mad at her.

9. *I Loved Him but Monogamy Wasn't For Me*

Calliope wrote down the names of all the men she had sex with. On her thirtieth birthday she sat on her porch, smoking a cigarette and counting the names. In fourteen years she had been sexual with fifty-three men, some only once, some a few times and a handful she shared ongoing sexual assignations with over the years. She loved sex and men and did not feel love had anything to do with sex. Sex felt good, relaxed her and she was safe, so why shouldn't she. The world was telling her that now she was married she should never have sex with another man and she didn't know if Calvin shared those thoughts or not but two years into the marriage and five months after having twins, she craved sex with another man.

It certainly wasn't because Calvin didn't satisfy her sexually, there was almost nothing they had not shared in that way and when she was in his arms, she never thought of another man. It was the times she was alone or with the children or walking in a store or somewhere, she would get a scent in her nose that filled her with yearning for the size, shape, feel and taste of a different penis. For two years she had not given in to the desire but now it was chasing her and it was an itch she knew only sex with another man would fill. Her mind flitted back to meeting Calvin three years earlier.

Standing in the smoky room, she puffed on her cigarette wondering who would take her home that night, rather who she would follow home. There were several choices in the room she knew would give her what she craved but when Calvin caught her eyes, she knew she wanted him. She knew exactly who he was. He coached football at the local high school and at forty was thirteen years older than her twenty-seven. She also knew women loved him and he was quite the ladies' man and a catch. He owned several acres outside of town and trained and bred horses as something he loved and as something that added significantly to his bottom line. Calliope admired entrepreneurs, being one herself. She owned a high-end thrift shop and was also an organizer, which meant she went into others homes or offices and for money taught them how to declutter and organize their spaces.

Calvin winked at her but didn't make a move, so she snuffed out her cigarette and made her way to him.

"Hello, Calvin Jones." She said.

"Hello Calliope Closets or is Closets not your last name?" He responded and made her laugh. Desire shot through her, funny men always made her wet. Getting closer to him, she could feel his heat. Calvin wasn't fat but was big like the former linebacker he was.

"I am Calliope Reynolds. However, Calliope Closets is me. Are you having fun or would you like to take me home? His eyes searched hers before answering.

"I am having fun and will only go home with you if you can promise it will be more fun than this."

Leaning further into him, she whispered, "I guarantee it."

She followed him to her place and tried to lead but Calvin proved to be forceful and handled her. She wasn't used to being handled. She tried climbing on top, telling him that was better for her orgasms. His response was she had been making love to the wrong men. Turns out he was right because he provided orgasms from all positions and his stamina was remarkable. After the sex she found him to be smart in addition to being funny and honest.

~~YYYYY~~

For months they were together and seeing others. Calliope was actually having sex with Calvin and another man until she wasn't. After a year when Calvin confessed having fallen in love with her, she admitted she was also in love. However when he proposed she wavered being honest in saying she didn't know if she could be sexually faithful no matter how much she loved him. She recalled his words.

"Have you ever loved anyone more than me or had better sex?"

She admitted she had done neither. What she didn't admit was it wasn't about better sex for her but different sex. She just sometimes wanted a different penis. They got married and had twins a year later, two boys they both adored.

However, after years of monogamy, Calliope wanted a different penis and she wanted Calvin too. He was her husband, lover and friend, but there was one thing he could not offer and that was a different penis.

~~YYYYY~~

Calliope stood watching the deliveryman unload the boxes through the back door. She was opening in two hours and the twins were with the sitter. Since giving birth she ran the shop three days a week, taking Wednesday, Saturday and Sunday off. Initially she brought the babies in with her but found she was too busy to work and take care of them. She had a part-timer who came in from two to six and she usually worked nine until about three thirty. When he was done, the deliveryman

166

turned to her and she smiled at him. His name was Harold and they enjoyed a temporary thing before she married Calvin.

"Ms. Calliope, is that it?" He asked, his eyes assessing her.

"Not really, about ten or fifteen minutes of your time would be nice." He knew exactly what she meant and grabbed her, pushing her over the desk, removed her underwear, sheathed his penis and thrust into her. She gave into the sensation of him and the newness of something yet familiar. Within fifteen minutes, he was on his way and she whistled as she worked. Something inside her was calmed and she could focus. The itch that had been burning and churning for days was abated.

That evening Calvin came home to her preparing food and the children were washed, fed and sleeping. She was dressed in a clingy, long dress he loved. Walking up behind her, he wrapped his arms around her, biting her neck, eliciting a moan.

"Woman, you look good, like you never had two babies. There is something extra special about you today."

Stepping back, she looked up at him with twinkling eyes.

"How special?" she murmured.

"Relaxed and blooming. The last few days you seem removed, almost as if you were in pain but I know you don't care for inquiries about how you are doing."

Chuckling, she dipped a spoon in sauce, holding it to his mouth to taste. He groaned at how good it was.

"That is so good but I want to taste your sauce. Turn off that stove and come with me. I know we have a couple of hours."

She did as he asked, allowing him to pick her up and carry her to their bedroom. Where he feasted on her before making hard love the way she sometimes craved it. Her earlier liaison was free from her mind. It was as if it never happened and she was free and whole with her husband.

If Calvin noticed anything different he didn't mention it and they enjoyed dinner and a few hours with their children after dinner.

YYYYY

Over the next six months, Calliope had three other encounters, with three guys and felt in her spirit she was being greedy and needed to self-check.

There had been nothing from Calvin to indicate he suspected anything.

The evening of her most recent assignation, she received a call on the way home from Calvin telling her he was going out and would be in later. She was surprised by that because Calvin was home most days by five, and usually worked on his horses on Fridays and Saturdays in the morning hours.

"Is everything okay?" she asked.

"Things are great. Kiss the boys for me and don't hold dinner." He said.

"You will be that late?" she asked.

"I'm not sure. I love you Calliope."

The call ended and she placed the phone on the seat but her head was awash with the change in Calvin. There was no inflection in his voice but she felt something was different.

After arriving home and getting the boys ready, she prepared salad for herself and when the boys slept, she dozed off. She startled awake at the sound of the alarm resetting and glanced at the clock and was surprised to discover it was almost midnight. After glancing at the boys, she stretched and made her way to the kitchen where she found Calvin standing in the refrigerator gulping down a glass of water.

"Hey." She said. Turning to her, he smiled tiredly. "Where have you been?" she asked.

"I was having sex with Marjorie." He said and held her gaze. Her belly quivered and the hair stood up on the back of her neck.

171

"Who is Marjorie and why were you having sex with her?" she asked, her voice trembling.

"She is someone I used to know and I was having sex with her because when we met I was having sex with her and you were having sex with others. Now you are doing it again, I figured I would as well. Calliope we are equal partners in everything. You insisted on paying your half once we were married and everything else is split so I figured since you were fucking, I should fuck too." His voice was calm and monotone. Pure blind fear filled her and chilled her.

"But Calvin..."

"But Calvin what? I should love you so much that it is okay to know when my wife is with another man and pretend I don't know her and her moods and what her body is like after sex with another

172

man... I do love you Calliope, I do but I am human and it is painful to know my wife needs another man or men to be satisfied."

"Calvin, no one satisfies me like you and when I'm with you, it's all you. It is just that I have always had these urges and desires and it is like they drive me until they are satisfied but they have nothing to do with loving you or my satisfaction with you..." she said and lowered herself into a chair. It was as if the air was suddenly sucked from her very spirit. "I always had this insatiable craving for random penises and it lasts all of ten minutes and then... that was why I thought I would never marry anyone."

"Calliope, we all crave things but when we take vows we honor them by finding ways to quell them. I don't know what that would take for you but you need to find it. By the way I didn't really have sex with Marjorie but that was my intention.

After insulting her by backing out, I drove around. I am not able to do this any longer."

Fear filled her right after she felt the relief of him not having been with anyone else. She knew that was wrong considering but her feelings were real ones. She did not want him sexual with others, which was too much to swallow and digest.

"Are you going to leave me?" she asked.

"I don't want to but I will..." was his answer.

"There are pills..."

"Like I said, you need to do whatever it takes but I will not and cannot do this. I know I should have said something the first night, instead I thought I could make it go away with our lovemaking but I know it happened again. Our marriage will not survive this. I need to check on the children and get some rest."

After he was gone, she checked the drawers in the kitchen and found a pack of cigarettes and figured out what she was going to do. She loved Calvin and tonight was proof of how much. In her late teens her mother had gotten wind of her habits and had gotten her a prescription that was actually an anti-depressant that worked with quelling her desires but it also slowed her down and after a couple of years she had stopped taking them but she knew now she would have to revisit that or lose the most important things.

YYYYYY

I met Calliope two years after her confrontation with her husband. She started counseling and the prescription and for the past two years had been faithful to her husband. She was a woman who oozed sexy with the way she stood and her mannerisms but it was not identifiable by any one thing, it just was who she inherently was. I will never forget our conversation after she gave me the background.

"How do you feel now?" I asked.

"I feel like someone other than who I am. I don't crave the new experiences but I really don't crave anything. My husband and I still have excellent sex but gone are the days when I was laying on the bed, waiting for him when he arrived home or the other spontaneous things I did sexually. In fact he almost always initiates sex these days."

There was something removed and matter of fact about what she was saying.

"Are you saying your senses have been dulled?" A wistful look flickered over her face before she answered.

"That's an excellent way to describe it."

"Does your husband notice it?" I asked.

"He has to, if he could tell when I had been with another man, surely he has noticed that. But that is the sacrifice we both made for love. I am not chasing the thrill of another penis inside me and he accepts that I am no longer as sexually adventurous or spontaneous. I could not stop it on my own. This was and is my survival tool. We all make sacrifices for love, don't we?"

Her words felt heavy to me and I felt her pain, though I completely and unequivocally understood why she did it and why her husband and marriage required it.

"We absolutely do." I said, some of my personal sacrifices flitting through my mind and the sacrifices that were made for me.

10.I Married Him Twice

Felicia would never forget the day he left her. It was raining hard but he insisted on taking his things to his truck in the downpour. Frederick always liked to make a point and his point was that he was leaving her and even the downpour couldn't stop him. They were married twenty-five years the day before and she literally forgot until now. Two months ago he asked her for a divorce and she accepted without arguing and he had the nerve to accuse her of never caring. Felicia was forty-six to his fifty-one. They had a son, aged twenty-three, who was incarcerated and Frederick had three children prior to the marriage. She was an adjudicator for social security and he worked until four months earlier as a driver for Winn Dixie grocery chain. A large part of their dysfunction had always been her ambition and education and his lack of the same.

Frederick worked hard but had never aspired to anything beyond driving a truck and education above high school had always seemed a waste to him. Felicia was two years out of college when they were married and had received a master's degree in finance at age forty. She worked for federal service and was GS-14 on the pay scale, which was as high as it was possible to go on that particular pay scale. The only thing she and Frederick enjoyed together was sex and the image they portrayed to outsiders. Inside their home had been filled with quiet or his derision for her and what he considered her uppity ways. She found it ironic he asked for a divorce when it was she who worked hardest to make things work. She prepared two meals a day, and kept their home sparkling clean in addition to bringing in two thirds of the household income. All they had was due to her ambition, saving and hard work. Let him go...

Thoughts of first meeting him filled her mind.

She noticed him immediately when he walked into the social security office. She was new and her trainer waited on him and an older man. It turns out the man was his father, who was applying for benefits. While the trainer assisted the father, Felicia felt his eyes on her and she returned his stare. He was handsome with a full mustache, a bit of an afro and well dressed. He looked sexy to her. When her coworker walked away to make copies he asked for her phone number and she hurriedly slid it across the desk. Other than asking that, they hadn't exchanged words. He nodded at her when they left.

Later that evening instead of calling, he showed up at her door.

"What are you doing here?" she asked, glad she hadn't changed from her work clothing. She was *sharing a place with a friend and was glad she wasn't home.*

"I figured it was just as easy to stop by. I thought maybe you would share your dinner with a lonely man. I am Fredrick Oliver and if you ask around town, you will find out I'm a decent man." Smiling a bit, she invited him in.

She was actually having leftovers but there was enough for him. She got him situated in the small sitting room before going to heat up the food, she didn't know him but was intrigued. When the food was done, she invited him to the kitchen and they chatted discovering they had friends in common and attended the same church. He was also forthright about his prior life where his ex and children were concerned.

"I was married and had two sons; the marriage broke up when I got another woman pregnant."

He said as he ate his food, staring at her. She wasn't impressed by that or his eating habits which involved slurping and chomping but she didn't say anything about that. She told him about her education and dreams and he didn't say much but complimented her on the food.

"You're a good cook. I guess you not one of those women who don't cook or clean." He said, glancing around the spotless home. "There are too many of those."

What he said bothered her but she didn't say anything because she was raised by a woman who felt just as her husband did. Her mom or sisters and brothers all claimed not to understand why she needed so much education. They asked her that in the late 1980s as if it were 1950.

After dinner he sat with her in the living room, getting close to her, touching her hair and being intimate and she was taken in by him. They didn't have sex that night but after a few weeks of him eating at her table, they did and she was addicted to his lovemaking. There were a plethora of other things about him she didn't care for and found him coarse in his language and habits but sex clouded her vision and within months they were married and two years later had a son.

The marriage was filled with rules for her and different ones for him from the start and because she had grown to love him, she acquiesced while quietly climbing the ladder at work. She also turned her son over to him because he accused her of pampering him and when he started getting in trouble it seemed too late to reach him. Frederick convinced her it was growing pains and being a boy until she stood across from a judge with him four years ago and watched him receive a twenty year sentence for drug trafficking. At that moment, *she saw her husband had changed but she still worked on the marriage.*

However, Frederick was no longer able to convince her to do things. She visited their son twice monthly and gave him money against Frederick's wishes and also helped care for a child their son sired. She started traveling for work as she was promoted and enjoyed her independence from Frederick and in her heart she knew that was part of why he was leaving. He no longer had control of her and felt, for unknown reasons she would expire without him. She knew she wouldn't.

Once the truck was filled Frederick walked back inside where she was sitting at the dining room table working on a scrapbook, one of her hobbies that he ridiculed.

"Good luck Felicia and maybe your next man won't need a real woman and will put up with you." He said. She didn't look up from her tasks.

"Please leave the key... no don't. I will get the locks changed." He threw the keys on the floor and walked out, allowing the door to slam. He had tried to get her to sell the house and share the proceeds but she had won the house and would continue to pay the mortgage. She had also received a third of his lump sum retirement due to the number of years they were married. He had fought that and lost.

~~ΥΥΥΥΥ~~

For nearly three years, Felicia enjoyed her freedom. She traveled a lot for work and had several flings with an ex from college and a few other guys but nothing ever felt workable. She was also facing fifty and wanted more than to spend her later years bed hopping. She had not met one man she wanted to marry or who asked to marry her. More so, none had been as good or as inventive in bed as Frederick. She saw Frederick in church and around town and periodically hear things about this woman or that one but there had been no communication until the night he showed up on her doorstep much the way he had almost thirty years earlier. She was startled when she opened the door and he was standing on the porch.

"Fred?" he looked at her sheepishly.

"Hey, I was just dropping by and wondered if you cooked something. I could swear I smelled your pork chops and sweet potatoes from down the road." He said.

"You don't smell that here. I just got home. What do you really want? Did you discover I am the only woman in the peninsula who still cooks?" He surprised her by laughing boisterously as he sat down on the covered iron bench, pulling off his hat. Closing the door, she stepped out on the porch. She didn't trust herself to invite him in because she was in need of lovemaking and he looked as good to her as ever and it had been months since a man was inside her.

"You still got that smart mouth." He said, his eyes roaming over her. Felicia was always body conscious and as she had gotten older she was even more careful about her food intake and she walked daily before work and at lunch. She was wearing a fitted dress that showed her figure. "You look real good too. Like honey." He said huskily and her insides thrummed with desire.

"Since you don't have any food, let's go down to the diner and get something." They had eaten so many meals at the diner over the years. He wasn't partial to what he called the fancy restaurants she liked and knew she did enjoy the diner but she wasn't in the mood for that.

"Actually, I was going to Seasons 52 for dinner. I love their shrimp and grits." He didn't know what Seasons 52 was but it sounded fancy but she was right. He had not found another woman like her out there and he wanted to come home. He had also been wrong about how well she would do without him. She had been promoted to the GM pay scale in the government and was driving a new car and had gotten work done on the house. He was living in a rundown place off Main Street and had long since lost the early retirement money. He invested in a trucking business with a friend and in short order the money and the friend was gone. He lost more than ninety thousand dollars. He wasn't old enough for social security and had gone back to work, driving the school bus.

"Okay, that sounds good. Let me take you." She glanced at his truck and told him she would meet him there in an hour. She walked inside and closed the door. Desire was overtaking her and what she wanted was for him to come inside and give it to her hard and go home.

Frederick smiled inside, thinking, at least she didn't say no.

He was not thrilled by her twenty dollars entree and a steak was thirty dollars and that didn't include drinks and desserts but he was going to ride it out. She watched him and was surprised when he didn't flinch at the menu and something in her uncurled. In the past he would have argued vehemently right in the restaurant. They ate dinner and chatted about people they collectively knew.

"I missed you Felicia. I love you. There is no woman out there like you." She didn't respond but after dinner she invited him in and they made love for the remainder of the weekend. They didn't leave the bed except for her to prepare meals.

When she told her son two months later she was considering allowing his dad to return home, he surprised her with his words.

"Mama, you are a grown woman but dad is a user. He will let you take care of everything and when the bottom falls out he is nowhere to be found. Trust me I know."

She heard her son but lust, residual love and loneliness led her to the justice of the peace to remarry him, again.

YYYYY

The first sign that a mistake had reoccurred was mere weeks into the marriage when he asked to be added to her checking account. When she refused, he confessed he had spent all his money and was working for ten dollars an hour.

"I am sorry to hear that Frederick, but I can't do that. You left here with almost a hundred thousand dollars and now you don't have it. What you earn is enough for you. I have paid off the house and all I have is monthly bills and my car. You will have to live off what you earn. You will also have to pay utilities and cable, both is two hundred a month."

"You are my wife and you have to share what you have with me!"

"No I do not. If we were living as you say we should, I would not have a job and you would be supporting me. If what you earn isn't enough, get another job."

Felicia had significant savings in addition to her 401K and other investments and was not going to allow him to blow through it. She just wasn't. She also was not going to allow him to manipulate her as he once had. She knew that as long as they were married he didn't have a leg to stand on but if they were ever divorced he would at a minimum be entitled to part of her retirement when she retired in a few years. What the hell had she done for a roommate and great sex? She wondered.

YYYYY

Sitting across from her two years after remarriage I must have looked dumbstruck by what she was saying. There was nothing in me that could relate. When she told me of the remarriage, I congratulated her and moved on. I genuinely thought she had made a good decision for her. I knew her as a savvy, got it going on woman and just knew how she handled her marriage was no different. We had never really discussed that because most of our connection had been through others. On that day she saw me eating alone and asked to join me and she shared as if we had been lunching and chatting forever.

"You are shocked aren't you?" she asked.

"Umm, yes." My response made her chuckle.

"Why?"

"Because you guys look like any other happy couple at church. There has been nothing to indicate otherwise. I didn't even know you had been divorced until you told me you were remarrying." She looked as if she didn't believe me.

"No one told you?"

"No. People don't tell me things like that. Your marriage never came up in a conversation I was in. Not only that, but until recently we were church members in passing."

"That's true." She said. "But people say a lot about you. Mostly that you are a counselor and mentor and you don't gossip. I guess that's why folks don't tell you stuff." I raised my fork.

"Anyway, I made a huge mistake. I am retiring next year and I am remarried to a man who married me the second time for money, sex and meals and someone to do his laundry and clean his house."

"Are you calling that man a gold-digger?" I said trying to make light. She wrinkled her nose at me.

"I guess so but I am not giving him my money."

"Is the money worth the misery?" I asked, seriously.

"I am not doing it. I made a horrible mistake allowing him back. I was horny and lonely and the guys out there would sex me but they weren't interested in much else."

"One should never make life decisions either horny or hungry. You should have asked him before the marriage about things like money, etc. And I know this sounds cold but considering all you should have made him sign a prenuptial the second time. You have saved a lot of money and will have a significant retirement of which he will get a portion if you divorce him. You are smart and educated Felicia."

"I know... I messed up."

"Is the sex even still good?" I had to ask.

"It is but he withholds that sometimes. I am a fool."

I didn't have anything to offer. I just didn't because she was a fool, a horny fool that got bitten by the same dog twice. I would likely let him have the money and move on. I mean they were in their fifties with lots of life left to live and living in misery for an occasional orgasm seemed just above my head.

"I am not sure what you want me to say..."

"I know what you want to say. I guess I just love venting."

"You could start a reality series?" I offered.
"When Brilliant Women do Dumb Womanish..."

She howled with laughter. I guess that was my part in all that, to provide comic relief.

I would love to say she made great decisions for her life but I cannot say that and that is based entirely on what I consider a great decision. They are still living together in the remarriage and getting from day to day. We all survive our Womanish differently.

11. He Was The Better Choice

Bobby was the love and desire of Winda's heart.
He made her smile by showing up and curled her
toes with kisses and his dark, masculine presence.
Norman however was her choice. Norman had all
the things she was supposed to want, an education,
a career and a sterling future and was from the
same kind of solid and hardworking family she
was spawned from. But he didn't make her heart
race or her panties wet. All he offered was him and
his love.

Bobby not once promised to love her or offer her
anything other than the time he shared with her
and the pleasure he filled her with that felt good
down to her bone marrow. He was also from
nowhere and everywhere. He barely graduated
high school and worked odd jobs supporting his
ventures and hustles but it didn't matter to her, she
had sat in many basements and garage apartments

listening to him and his friends perform great music no one would ever likely purchase. But for him that didn't seem to matter, his focus more than anything seemed to be to not be mediocre. He said the word as if it were filthy in his mouth. She wanted him.

But at twenty-nine she was tired of waiting for Bobby and when Norman arrived in town to run the bank, she accepted his offer to go out. She was teaching as a master teacher and wanted more than smoky basements and great sex on a mattress on the floor. She wanted children, a husband, and a life. She recalled her words to Bobby about going out with Norman.

"Ma, if that's what you want, I think you should go for it. I am not ready to offer you that. I am still getting my life together and I am not bringing any little shorties in this world." He said standing before her looking impatient, looking like the

chocolate god she had grown to love more than she loved herself. "Do you." He turned from her and went back to his work. For the first time, she walked out and away. She didn't see him look after her with surprise but neither did he follow her. The next night she went out with Norman.

Opening the door for her, Norman handed the keys to the valet driver and led her inside the spacious restaurant. It had been open for four years and still getting rave reviews but Winda had only ever been there with her friends or coworkers. She and Bobby never ate out because he couldn't afford to and when he earned money it either went into the music or on his back. Bobby was always stylish and his equipment top of the line, though he didn't have a real home or steady employment.

"I'm surprised you agreed to dinner Winda. I was after you for years before leaving here but your mind was on other things. My mom said you are

201

doing well as a master teacher, what is that
exactly?" He asked with interest.

She focused on Norman realizing Norman was an
attractive man who was very well groomed, even if
he was a bit heavier and shorter than what usually
appealed to her.

"It means I am a teacher with a master's degree in
my educational field which is math. We earn
twenty percent more than most teachers and
receive bonuses. It is great, not as great as
teaching at the college level but comparable. I love
teaching." His eyes smiled at her answer and she
realized it felt good to talk to a man who was
genuinely interested in what she did or was doing.
"That's great; we need teachers who care about
kids and education. Do you volunteer?" He asked.

"I do. I actually have paid and unpaid
volunteerism work beyond my career. I also work

ten hours a week for She Counsels. That's a non-profit that tutors and pays well. That is my investment money and two afternoons a week I tutor at my old high school assisting young mothers catch up on math skills for graduation and testing purposes." He smiled and she responded to his smile with one of her own.

The waiter came and they ordered and discussed volunteerism and work over dinner. She now knew what her friends meant about being 'wined and dined.' No one had taken her out since she returned from college and got involved with Bobby. Or, re-involved because she had been with him in high school.

After dinner they walked down to the river where there were jazz bands playing for donations. Norman had actually reserved an area for them that was secluded right on the water with a bottle of wine.

"Winda, are you involved with anyone?"

"No, I am as free as I can be. Are you?"

"No. As you know, I just returned. I wasn't really focused on that until now. I wanted to run my own bank by thirty-five and here I am five years early. A brother is now thinking of settling down." His eyes met hers. *"You never stopped being on my mind. I would like to see you, get to know you."* He said softly. Her answer was to sit a bit closer to him.*

~~ΫΫΫΫ~~

After making up her mind to date Norman, Bobby stopped by a few times but she stuck to her resolve and told him she was involved. Her heart was with him but she needed to do better. Bobby not ever being a man lacking for feminine attention moved on with his life. They ran into each other occasionally and she was usually with Norman.

She recalled the first incident after she and Norman were dating about six months. There was an indie music festival they attended downtown and Bobby was one of the headliners. She sat stoically beside Norman not trying to show the raging emotions she felt. Bobby was an excellent performer and musician and that night he was performing without his shirt. She and Norman had a decent sex life but nothing like the raw, gritty sex she enjoyed with Bobby. Her mom and friend had convinced her that grown up sex got better and that sex paid no bills. After the set, Norman took her hand and made his way to Bobby. The two men graduated together.

"Great job man. I see you are the hometown man." Norman said. Bobby smiled and pulled on his t-shirt.

"Is that you or me, man? You are the one running things and making all the moves." Bobby said, his eyes flickering over Winda before returning to meet Norman's. Feeling suddenly chilled, Winda moved closer to Norman.

"No, it's definitely you man, sticking to what you believe in and doing your thing." Norman said. "Great work."

Winda expected Norman to say something condescending after they walked away but he didn't and picked up a few CDs before they walked down the pier for dinner. He had never mentioned Bobby since their initial date. That was one of the things she was growing to love about Norman, he didn't knock the next man; he simply did his own thing. Bobby had always called men like Norman sellouts.

It came as no surprise to anyone that one year after they started dating Norman proposed and Winda accepted. She loved him and knew he loved and was in love with her and he offered her solidity.

Two days before the wedding, Norman was away for an overnight and Winda sat alone eating dinner at a local restaurant when Bobby dropped in a chair across from her. He was a handsome as ever and a faint scent of hemp and lavender surrounded him. Looking up from her salad, she glanced at him and saw something in his eyes she never saw, it looked suspiciously like pain.

"Don't do it Winda." He said.

"Do what Bobby?"

"Don't marry that dude. I know you think it's the best thing for you but I know you love me and I love you. I didn't say it or show it enough but I do. I just got a job working almost full time..." She shook her head at his words.

"Are you kidding me right now, Bobby? It has been over a year and two days before I get married you expect me to just give back this ring and break the heart of a man who adores me so I can hop on the back of your bike. That is not happening."

"You will be happy with me. We were good together. The music thing is going better and with this job, in a couple of years..." She held up her hand for him to see the significant sized ring.

"Bobby, I am getting married now."

She dropped money on the table and strode to her car. Bobby jumped on his motorcycle and followed her home. She didn't see him until he pulled up when she was at her door. Grabbing her, he covered her mouth with his and kissed her with pent-up passion. She wanted to refuse him but her body didn't and she gave in to the feelings she missed and craved.

Afterwards she rolled over in bed and asked Bobby to go. He sat up, looking down at her.

"Winda, you want this and not that."

"Bobby, I might want this but I need that. Please go and don't dream of messing this up for me. Just go."

After he left she cried herself to sleep. Not sure what she was crying for.

Two days later she was married and spent two weeks in Japan on her honeymoon.

Three weeks later she announced to the world she was one month pregnant with their first child.

YYYYY

For three years Winda and Norman worked, loved and lived, raising their son, Norman II. Norman wanted another child but they were not getting pregnant and it wasn't for lack of trying. Winda convinced him that maybe God only meant for them to have one son. Norman II was the spitting image of Winda, though a bit darker in complexion than she was and considerably darker than Norman.

"I guess we are gifted with one child. It is just as well, I am almost thirty-five and we are blessed with him but don't stop trying." Norman asked and Winda nodded in agreement. She had always been concerned that the one night with Bobby might have been when she got pregnant but Norman II was born nine months and one day after her marriage. Norman II didn't look at all like Norman, but neither did he look like Bobby, but he was just like Norman in his mannerisms and loved being on the golf course and soccer field with his daddy. He was theirs.

Within months after marrying Norman, Winda heard Bobby moved to Miami and was doing well there with his music career. There had been a modest selling album the year before and many spoke of his hectic touring schedule. She was happy for him but hadn't seen him in over two years with no intention to see him. Norman had other plans.

"We are going where?" Winda asked; her heart racing.

"To the Center. It seems Bobby Wilkerson is performing and he's an old friend. We should support him."

Winda felt faint. The last person she wanted to see was Bobby. Out of sight and mind had been just fine for her. Well, out of sight.

"When did you become a big consciousness music person?" Winda snapped.

Norman's brow rose. Winda was the most even keeled person. She was patient with him, Norman II, who could be a brat, and her students.

"Are you kidding? I often hung out with Bobby and his crew before college and sometimes on breaks. But after college I had goals and business. We are going. I hear he's finally getting heard. He was always about his music. I'm proud." Winda literally wanted to refuse but could see no way out.

The Center held fifteen hundred people and was filled to the rafters. It was, according to Norman, the fifth sold out performance of Bobby's that month. She and Norman were dressed as they always were; high end chic. Her dress was snug and fitted and her heels high and her formerly natural hair flowed sleekly to her shoulders. Bobby wore baggy jeans and his usual fine cotton shirt with cuff links and Ferragamo shoes. They looked like money. Real money that was earned; saved and invested before shopping and that's who they were. Their seats were excellent and near the front. Inside Winda's heart raced and when Bobby took the stage she felt faint. He looked the same except thirty extra pounds of muscle and beard that added something special. For ninety minutes, his flow was impeccable and the crowd, including Norman rocked with him. After the concert there was wine and mingling. Winda wanted to leave but Norman wasn't having it. They were sitting and sipping when Bobby glided in followed by a thick bodied but fit fashionista with a huge fro, flawless skin and eyes fastened on Bobby. They made their way to their table and Norman stood shaking his hand and congratulating him. Winda had a smile pasted on her face and wasn't prepared for the impact Bobby had on her when he focused those lazy eyes on her. She felt as if he saw all her secrets and the desires of her heart.

"Hello Wind." He used his pet name for her. "Marriage and motherhood is good to and for you" He said. "This is my girl Janae, Janae; these are my people from home." Janae offered her hand and assessed Winda. Winda felt as if Janae knew her. "I appreciate y'all coming out. My folks will get you some swag." Bobby said before walking off with Janae on his heels. Winda finally exhaled.

"He's doing big things. Good for him. I think that's his lady." Winda didn't utter a word but swallowed down her wine and excused herself. As luck would have it she ran into Bobby who stopped her.

"Winda, you really look good. I'm surprised by the chemical hair but it suits you. I'm glad you're happy." She didn't respond and they stared at each other until Janae walked out the restroom and Winda fled inside. She sat inside the stall several minutes controlling her feelings. Bobby still entranced and unnerved her. After using the restroom and dabbing her face she made her way back to her husband, the man she chose. She kissed him on the mouth and told him she was hungry. Smiling at her, he stood, kissing her back before taking her for dinner and back to their son and life.

YYYYY

To me, Winda was the ultimate go-getter who had husband, child, home, faith and made a difference in the community. I admired what she and her husband were about but he always seemed happy in her presence but to me she seemed more resigned and content than happy. She seemed like many women, doing what they had to do. During a volunteer activity, that we both showed up for and wasn't needed, I invited her for coffee. She readily agreed and revealed herself more by happenstance then anything. It was several months after Bobby's concert but on that day he walked into the coffee shop. Spotting us, he made his way over. I stood to embrace him; I had seen him grow up. After hugging me, he turned to Winda and her face was transformed. I had never seen such naked love on a woman's face. She quickly masked it.

"What's up Winda? No hugs..." He said lightly. Winda stood and lightly hugged him but he wrapped his arms around her before stepping back and touching her hair. It was a mass of curls. "I see you went back home with your hair. Looks good."

When he turned to me and walked away, I saw the same open love on his handsome face. Within minutes, he was leaving as if he had called in his order. When he was gone, she turned to me, tears on her lids. I handed her a napkin and she told me the entire condensed story including the slim chance Norman II was Bobby's.

"Do you love Norman?" I asked, finally.

"I do love him. He's my husband, lover and best friend. He's the best man and I would never hurt him."

"But your heart is still consumed with Bobby and you feel if you had only waited you would be with him and filled with nightly passion and excitement." She snorted at my dry tone.

"You make it sound silly."

"I'm not trying to do that. However, we all have the one who got away that we wonder about. It's called life. What you have to do is weigh what you have against what you might have and decide what's best for you and spend lots of time in prayer. I'm proud of you and your husband and I'm proud of Bobby. The thing is reality and fantasy doesn't always add up as we like."

"I'm not a dumb woman, I chose my husband and I'm not leaving him. I just don't want to be judged because a part of me, my heart will always be there."

Taking her hands, I held them between mine.

"No judgment here, now stop judging yourself. Live the life you chose. It looks like a blessed one."

"It really is. Thank you."

Four months later I saw her with her husband and son and she looked like something had relaxed in her. She rushed into my arms, telling me she was eight weeks pregnant. In that moment I understood she had been carrying a bigger albatross than just having a bit of her heart with another man.

Her husband joined us and I congratulated him. He turned to her with love-filled eyes.

"I'm a blessed man."

"You're also a blessing." I said before hugging her to my heart and heading home to my blessed choices. We all make them.

12. *My Life Was Better After He Died*

Vernita married Orvis when she was twenty and he was twenty-two. He was working as a mechanic and she sold sandwiches at a stand near the Chevrolet dealership where he worked. She could not point to a physical thing that attracted him to her because he wasn't tall and he was very slender and always had a cigarette hanging out the side of his mouth. But there was something about the way he looked straight at her, the way his cap was always rakishly appointed and how women always hung around him. Orvis was from a good family but he was the never do well baby boy of five children and it wasn't because he didn't work, he had a good job. It was because he drank hard liquor, spent time in clubs with fast women and he didn't seem to allow much to bother him. Vernita's family were simple hardworking people who spent their times working, at church and working and they kept tight rein on their girl children. They certainly didn't want her messed up with the likes of Orvis but from the first night he waited for her after work, he could have gotten her to day anything.

She was startled when she walked into the alley and Orvis was leaning up against the wall smoking a cigarette. He was still wearing his uniform that looked fresh with a sparkling white baseball cap. He stood up straight and smashed out the cigarette with the heel of his boot.

"What are you doing here Orvis?" Vernita asked trying to keep the excitement out of her voice. He had teased her daily the last year since she started working there and he always left her a dollar tip even if his order didn't come too much.

"I came to propose marriage but since it's too soon, I will just walk you home."

His words curled inside her belly and she wrapped her arms around her waist as if to hold them inside. A block from her house, he stopped pulled her near a huge oak tree and kissed her with passion. For the first time in her life she knew what it meant to blossom.

"Open your mouth baby and let your tongue dance with mine." He whispered and she did. He took his time teaching her to kiss. Finally, pulling her way he walked her home and stood in the shadows until she got inside. He knew the very religious Tylers would not approve of him with their pure daughter but he had been serious about wanting to marry her. He felt she was just the kind of woman to give him stability. He needed stability.

They continued the walks and kisses until the night they arrived at her house and Mr. Tyler stood on his porch with a suitcase filled with Vernita's

clothing. He didn't look at his daughter but
addressed Orvis.

"You have ruined my child and now she is yours,
you can marry her and try to repair her reputation
or you can continue sneaking around with her and
turn her into a common woman." He dropped the
suitcase and walked inside. They could hear him
bolting the locks. Vernita turned to Orvis in shock.

"What am I going to do, where am I going to go?"
She asked.

"I will take you to my sister's and as soon as we
can we will get married. I have a small house for
us." Picking up her bag, he led her to his sister's
and four days later they were married without
benefit of any family except the sister who took her
in, a few of her coworkers and his friends.
Immediately there was a pattern to their lives, he
worked and brought home most of his money and

she took care of the house, paid the bills, had sex with him when he wanted it, which was most nights, and she had babies.

~~YYYYY~~

By the time Vernita was twenty-seven and Orvis twenty-nine they had five children under the age of six and she looked like an older woman caring for him and their children in the same tiny house. They would never as long as he was alive, move to a bigger place. Orvis actually made great money but what he kept for himself went on alcohol, gambling and she suspected other women. There were rumors there were also other children out there he fathered but she never knew. She had reunited with her family and was back in the church, seeking from that what she didn't receive from her husband and no matter what that is who he was. Every morning she prepared his meals and kept his food warm no matter how late he returned home and never once did she refuse him sex. She needed that as much as he did. He was still his solid place. The only reason she didn't have more children is because the doctor advised her not to.

For fifteen years their lives were a routine that never varied other than the children getting older and her thinner and older. Orvis hadn't aged a day and when someone from Chevrolet came to tell her he died on the job at thirty-seven, she was shocked into a trancelike state. For the first several days, someone else had to care for her children aged fourteen to nine. Orvis's sister filled in and took care of her until almost two weeks later when it was time to bury her husband. She got out of bed dressed in black and stood with her children and family at Orvis' graveside funeral. He had never stepped foot inside a church and she didn't see the point in taking him to one after he died. The night of the funeral, she recalled sitting quietly as people expressed their condolences and the children ventured in and out of the tiny home, not really understanding Orvis was gone forever. She knew if it didn't make sense to her, it certainly wouldn't to them.

Three days later she felt as if her life flipped on its side. She was called into a local attorney's office where they told her that Orvis had money left from his job, and since he died at work, she would receive forty percent of his earnings until she died unless she married again. The amount stunned her because the forty percent was more than he gave her weekly to run that house. She was also told she would receive social security benefits for each of her children because her husband paid into the system. For several minutes she couldn't speak. For two days she wondered at night how she would feed her children and all of a sudden she had a few thousand dollars a month in non-taxable income and enough in a lump sum to purchase a home, something she stopped thinking of years earlier. Laughter bubbled up in her and she was unable to control it. The attorney glanced at Lois, Orvis' sister who knew her brother well and completely understood Vernita's hysteria.

YYYYY

For more than three months Vernita woke early in the morning and prepared food for the children sending them to school before slowly getting rid of the broken bits of furniture in their home and replacing it. She also did the same with the children's clothing. Everything they owned before Orvis died was from the thrift shops and or she made them. They only got new things at Christmas and very few. Lois and the attorney didn't understand what she was doing but she knew and couldn't be swayed. After doing that, she sat quietly studying homes in the newspaper until it was time to prepare food for her children.

During the evenings she talked to them about school and other things before allowing them to watch the new television she purchased. Before that they owned a small black and white Orvis already owned with a fuzzy picture. He always told her there wasn't money for a new one. She also told and retold them how much their daddy loved them, recreating an image in their minds.

On the ninetieth day after the kids left she caught a cab and drove to the real estate office on Forest Street and told the receptionist she wanted to purchase a house on Magnolia. It was a house she always admired and it was older, sturdy with three floors. They tried to sway her to another home that was more modern and newer but her mind was made up. She wanted that home on the huge lot with gigantic old trees and it wouldn't eat up all her money. She would be able to furnish it, work on it and still have money. It was also a home that had formerly been owned by well to do white folks and she wanted her and her kids to have it. She couldn't articulate it but it was the late 1980s and she didn't have to. She knew her kids had been ridiculed for their clothing and where they lived and she was going to assure that never happened again. They were in fourth to ninth grades and their lives would change. Orvis did for them in death what he never did in life. He made all of their lives better. The truth was though, she missed him day and night, especially at night because she knew he was no one's idea of a good husband or even man but he had been hers, and when it was just the two of them in that tiny room, all was well in her life.

YYYYY

Within a year after Orvis' death Vernita was barely recognizable. Gone were the wigs and old lady dresses and in their place was a short haircut and modest stylish clothing. She also left the Pentecostal church of her upbringing for the more sedate African American Episcopal Church. Her children were flourishing in school and activities and in the evenings, she took night classes learning new things. She was currently enrolled in an upholstering class and the instructor was her lover. No one knew but the two of them. Many nights after the classes were over she would return and become her alter ego, the wanton V who allowed the younger and virile man to make love to her on the newly upholstered furniture they worked on. Weeks earlier, she surprised him by approaching him, saying, "I need a secret lover." When she stepped out of her clothing he was more than interested. V was also uninhibited and voracious the way she had been with Orvis but more so because she now understood her power.

YYYYYY

The next years of her life was filled with secret lovers by night and most appropriate behavior by day. If anyone ever discovered her night life they never mentioned it to her and the community always called on her for assistance. Vernita was considered a virtuous woman who raised good, respectable, hardworking children and never missed a church service. They also admired how she turned early widowhood into a great life. She also never said glowing things about her late husband. That was surely best considering he gave her the best life by dying.

Those were the first words she said to me after we were introduced.

"Excuse me."

"I said I had my best life after my husband died. I loved him until the day he died. I still love him but our overall life other than love and sex was a poor mess. He blessed me in death and I've lived happily ever after." I peered at her under my lashes and knew there was a story there but that day I didn't want to know. I suddenly was a woman just overfilled with other *Woman*Ish...